The Girl and the Goddess

Stories and Poems of
Divine Wisdom

NIKITA GILL

G. P. PUTNAM'S SONS
NEW YORK

PUTNAM
— EST. 1838 —

G. P. PUTNAM'S SONS
Publishers Since 1838
An imprint of Penguin Random House LLC
penguinrandomhouse.com

Copyright © 2020 by Nikita Gill

ISBN 9780593085660

Printed in the United States of America
1 3 5 7 9 10 8 6 4 2

Jai Ganesh.
Jai Saraswati.
Jai Parvati.
Jai Kali ma.
Jai Durga mata.

For us,
and all the prayers
that we believed
no one was listening to.

Characters in this book persevere through:

Anxiety
Bigotry
Biphobia
Body shaming
Bullying
Child abuse
Depression
Guilt
Homophobia
Internalised misogyny
Misogyny/sexism
Poverty
Racism
Sexual assault
Terrorism
Violence
War

Contents

Prastaav

Prologue

In This Story

There is a girl who is stubborn
and strong-willed and who makes
mistakes enough to fill an ocean.

A family that is trying to navigate
its way through the aftermath
of war and partition.

And a pantheon of
Gods and Goddesses who appear
seemingly at random.

So when magic comes to stay,
it brings with it
a firestorm of emotions.

A Secret from Me to You

There is a thing
You should know
before reading this tale.

Despite my best efforts,
I still do not know
how to love myself.

But here
is the secret
that no one told me.

It's okay.

It's okay to feel
like you're drowning
inside your own bones sometimes.

It's okay to weep
like a sky devoured
by a storm.

It's okay to be aware
that there are wounds in you still
that you aren't letting heal.

Survival is ugly.
Healing is messy.
Self-love is complicated.

It is your hardest days
as much as your best days
that help you grow.

All of this
is part
of being human.

You and I,
we do not need
to learn alone

when we can learn together.
How to be gentle with ourselves.
How to be kinder to ourselves,

especially when life feels
like it is more endings
than beginnings.

Here is another secret no one will tell you,
There aren't any masters of self-love,
not even the Gods and Goddesses themselves.

Bachpan

Childhood

*There are only
two kinds of magic
given to humans in this world.*

*One is love.
The other
is prayer.*

My Mother Makes Pilgrimage to Vaishno Devi Before I Am Born

The first time my mother practises her magic,
it is before the Goddess under her mountain's care.

With folded henna-covered hands and eyes closed,
she speaks about the child in her womb in prayer.

In a cave where everything is fragranced with water,
she asks for a daughter instead of praying for a son.

Asks for a girl with eyes so dark the moon herself
falls in love and begs to live within them.

Asks for a girl with hair as opaque as a myna bird's throat
when she first learns to speak-sing.

Let her be stronger, so much stronger than me.
Let this baby have your fearlessness, mother Goddess,

the same mettle, the same ease that you had
when you brought your enemies to their knees.

Let her be a little less human, a little more divine.
Give her heart armour so it doesn't break as easily as mine.

Give this to her, and she will no longer
be my child for I promise her to you.

We are a spiritual people.
When we make the long pilgrimage

to the mountain Goddess,
so many of our prayers come true.

Whether we are the masters of manifestation,
or our Gods really do listen, this I leave to you.

Wildest Wish

My mother, by the way,
got the wild daughter
she desired.

(Be careful what you wish for.
Sometimes the universe listens
like a child does to her parent.

Too intently.

Absorbing,
        absorbing,
                absorbing,

till it is ready to burst.

And the alchemy of that chaos
is what makes the worst version
of our best wish come true.)

The First Visit

When the Goddess first visits,
I am defined by my mother's voice,
but my father's silent nature.

I am a jigsaw this family
pieces together
each time they call.

My grandfather's nose.
My grandmother's cheeks.
My aunt's hands.

Everyone tries
to find themselves in me   → brown family expectations?
as if I am more mirror, less infant.

I am the first daughter
in six generations on my father's side,
the first child of the first children.

The Goddess cares for none of this
the night she leans over my cot,
hair flowing into my face like a night river.

Everything about her screams
silver storms and riotous rage,
but I am too young to know fear yet.

Her wide eyes bore into mine,
golden opulence at her ten wrists
and throat catching the moonlight.

Something nameless scented
of sulphur and jasmine sits between us
until her lips raise in a smile and she speaks.

'Everything about you
may look like someone else,
but that spirit was my gift to you
and no one else.'

She reaches into the cot,
lifts me up till I am facing the abyss.
'Come. It is time for you to hear the first story.'

The First Story

There are Gods that you know and Gods that you do not know. But they are the same Gods. This is the part of the story you must recognise before they teach you a different tale. Our creation is unique, as three Gods become our triumvirate. Call them Trimurti, the ancient Sanskrit word for 'three forms'.

Science names these forces something different. It calls them creation, maintenance and destruction.

But we are a more lyrical people, storytelling rises in our bones.

We named them Brahma, the creator; Vishnu, the preserver; and Shiva, the destroyer. Everything you learn will be about them, from Brahma's benevolence to Vishnu's divinity to Shiva's balance. You will go to temples and worship them, eat soft, sweet ladoos which are given by your temple pujaris as blessings until the sugar and prayer become one in your head.

These three Gods then created the heavens:

the Devas – other gods of the elements like the wind and fire and water,

and the Asuras – the demigods of both childlike good and bad intentions who are sometimes mistaken for demons.

But what they will not tell you is who both Gods and demigods fear. This is one of those stories. Beyond the realm of human, in the centre of the universe, there sits a golden forest. The trees rise higher than any planet has ever been graced with. The birds range from elegant mauve-feathered peacocks to eagles that can carry whole armies. Lions with emerald eyes and thick silver manes roar as blue gazelles with diamond eyes run across this metallic yet soft land. Now imagine the peace of this sacred ground disturbed by the violence of war. The platinum blood spilled of Gods killing their own.

This is where I was born.

We are arrogant beings. We believe in blessing those with boons who pray to us; but no one knows how to take boons back, and this is the greatest flaw of our universe. Brahma made one such mistake. A trillion years ago, before the Earth had breathed her first breath, an Asura named Mahisha prayed for immortality. Brahma, taken with his years of commitment to prayer, offered him a boon which stipulated he could have anything, just not immortality, for that was preserved for Gods alone.

Mahisha thought hard and asked, 'Then, Lord, if I can be killed, let it be at the hands of a woman and only a woman.' Mahisha thought himself clever, even cleverer than the Gods. Surely no mere woman could kill him. Brahma without another thought blessed the young demigod; and just like that, he signed the contract to a centuries-long war.

Mahisha's first action was to cause havoc. He took his tribe of demigods, single-handedly terrorised his cousins, the Devas, until they left their own abode.

At the end of their tether, the Devas approached Shiva, the destroyer, and begged him for his help. Through the power of the great God's prayer, from the ground of the golden forest I was raised. I became bigger and brighter in my crimson saree, the colour of blood reminding them all that women are used to violence from birth; we are born fierce in ways they can never understand. Gold dust was where my form began.

I arrived on my faithful, ferocious lion. My many arms, each holding a weapon, but Mahisha? He laughed and stated arrogantly, 'How could the Devas think I could ever be defeated by this simple woman.'

Now there is a stealth here, dear one. You must let your enemy underestimate you. When they do, each victory will be yours, for they will give you the blessing of surprising them with your courage, your brutality and your wisdom too.

When Mahisha lowered his defences, because he thought defeating me would be easy, I hit him with the force of nine Goddesses within me.

His army fell beneath all the women in me. His horses ran free. Still, he tried to change into a bull to try to defeat me. But I was brutal and violent in a way they tell women not to be. Through my ruthlessness, I brought an end to his life, with a single cut of my sword.

There is a reason why they say that the Devi is the most powerful of the Gods. Because when even the Gods could not save the universe from evil, it was the Devi that they called. This is why the Devi reincarnates as much as the Gods. This is how we keep balance restored.

As for the golden forest, it now lives within me. I swallowed it whole, so it can live on for eternity.

° Great testament to the power of women?

♭ we have a lot of inner strength!

After the Visit

The Goddess lays me back to sleep,
abyss eyes lingering on my tiny face.

With the sound of bangles jangling
and a thousand stars silently bursting,

she disappears from my sight.
Years later, my mother would ask me:

What was your first memory?
And I will remember:

a revolution of a woman
who swallowed a golden forest.

And not one of the hundred relatives
who had visited my cradle.

The First Word

It will happen like this:

The morning always begins
with prayers to Ganesh,
the elephant-headed God
with the single tusk.

The Kashmiri sun
then fills the room.
The family settles for breakfast
at the old mahogany table.

The radio plays songs
from Dev Anand films.
It is a soft, familiar
start to the day.

A table laid
with fruit and eggs
and paranthas, and love
and conversation.

A fractured family
that still knows
how to honour
the art of communication.

But today is different.
Today the baby, only six months old
and not yet meant to speak,
will say her first word.

'Allah.'

The One of Many Names

Maybe the ancients were right when they said God's test is hiding in everything we cannot explain. Maybe this is why when I am an infant, I say God's name first. I am too young to know the differences between religions. I am too young to understand religious tensions between Hindus and Muslims. My family is Hindu. We live in Kashmir. This means things. It is dangerous for everyone, no matter what faith we are, to feel safe here. Yet this is the only home we have all ever known. Once, long ago, we were all friends, neighbours, family to each other. Now old wounds paint the ground we live on crimson. Old grudges shape narratives into weapons of mistrust. But what do babies know about religious beliefs and warfare? Children are sponges, they say. They repeat what they hear. I say God's name because the most soothing voice I hear comes from a mosque close to this house we live in. Every morning a clear, dulcet voice wakes me from my childish dreams. It sends a prayer to my ears the moment I open my eyes.

Isn't that miracle enough?

Should it matter if the name spoken is Allah or Ganesh if your morning begins with God's name?

Mama

Mama is fire.
Is a Goddess without her powers
in a world of masculinity gone awry.
Is mystical despite them
trying to tell her she is not.

Mama is the second word I learn
though she is prouder of my first
because I named God.

Mama treats my father's parents
with kindness even though
they treat her with spitefulness.
Calls me her miracle
in a world that has let her down
with a thousand little indignities.
Reads me stories of Jhansi ki Rani
and the Goddess Durga
eliminating greed
before fairytales or Panchatantra.

Mama says, 'Paro, you will not
have to fight like I did
because I will fight for you.'
Says, 'I married a better man
than my father ever was
and I did it for you.
So you could grow.'

Mama doesn't let anyone
discipline me
under the premise of
'One day she will be a wife'.

Mama teaches me early:
'Despite what they will try to teach you,
Girl is not a dirty word.
Girl is power.

Girl is fury.
Girl is never-give-up-
the-world-cannot-break-me.'

Every Evening, We Watch the News

The news says:

'A clash with the army in Srinagar
has left seven people dead.
Two were children.'

And our picnic out
the next day
is cancelled.

The news says:

'A bomb scare has been
reported at Dal Lake.
Curfew from six tonight.'

And we have
to abandon our movie plans
for the evening.

The news says:

'Terrorists set off
two grenades killing eight
in Lahore.'

And Sania Auntie
no longer comes to visit
us any more.

The news says:

'We spoke to a father
who just lost
his daughter.'

The news says:

'All he wanted
was to say goodbye
to her.'

The father on the news says:

'We
pray for
peace.'

Just like my parents say:

'We
need
peace.'

Just like my grandparents say:

'Will we
ever
know peace?'

'Papa, What Is a Terrorist?'

Papa looks up from his book,
heavy brows furrowed.
'Where did you hear that word?'

I sway slightly from side to side,
my hands clasped in front of me.
'The man on the TV said it.'

'The presenter,' Papa corrects me,
then puts his book down
and rubs his eyes with his big hand.

After an age, he tells me,
'They're people who hurt other people
because of what they believe.'

I contemplate this.
'Are they bad people?'
There is a sadness in his eyes now.

I always know he's sad
when his eyes grow redder.
'They're hurt people,' he says, finally,

'and they've been taught
that the only way to overcome that hurt
is through hurting others.'

He looks me in my eyes,
"And you must never hurt an innocent
person just because you're hurt. Understand?"

I nod slowly. Silence sits between us,
the air heavy with the inexplicability
of death and grief.

'Go play, Paro,' Papa says finally,
'I'm going to finish my book.'
But when I turn to look at him,

he is staring out of the window,
the book abandoned on the table,
tears falling down his cheeks.

Childhood

The beauty of childhood is that
we are able to turn the mundane into magic.
Toys come to life when we aren't looking.
Kitchens are full of potion ingredients.
Gardens harbour fairy creatures.
We view our lives story-shaped
where happily ever after is guaranteed –
because the good people always win,
the bad people always lose,
and *we* are the good people, right?

That's just how it's supposed to be,

                                      isn't it?

No wonder they say children can survive anything.
We have not yet looked at life as a thing we can fail.

Rules

Mama says:
If you can finish your Rooh Afza milk fast enough,
you can go outside to play with Aafiya.

Not *too* fast because the sharbat
might make you throw up.

Dadi says:

Have you been playing in the mud
with the neighbour's daughter?

Stop it, Paro, they are not like us.
Look how dirty your clothes are.

Dada says:

She seems like a nice child,
but don't bring her home.

You know how your dadi feels
about the family next door.

Papa says:

Don't listen to either of them.
You make friends with whoever you want to.

All our hearts beat exactly the same
whether we are Hindu or Muslim.

Aafiya

If I were to describe something beautiful, I would describe the ly-chee tree in the garden, as abundant as a grandmother in its own way, whether by offering shelter or nourishment. Or maybe the moon. The moon, glimmering from the room I shared with my parents, my tiny bed close to the big window, because I liked to fall asleep looking at the stars. But the only person-shaped beautiful I knew was Aafiya. Wild forest-green eyes, and even wilder hair that looked like it didn't know a hairbrush, her smile always a little lopsided, a gap where her front tooth had fallen out, where her grown-up teeth hadn't come in yet. She only ever had one earring in and always gave a new reason why when I asked her about it. Today, she tells me a dog bit off the other one and laughs at the shock on my face. 'Paro,' she laughs, 'you are so easy to fool.' I blush and try to hide it with laughter of my own. Those days are all spent trying to make treasure troves out of flowers and fruit from the orchards. We play Rani-Rani, where we both get to be queens because we need no kings to rule our kingdom of stray puppies, herons, geese and fruit trees. We drag our fingers through the mud by the little stream to make another tiny stream and then another till each one glitters in the sun while we run, trying to wipe our hands on each other's kurtas. When I finally reach home, I always hide from my grandmother, but today is different.

Today, the house feels deathly still in the way my whole family is gathered in front of the television. Mama and Dadi hide their faces from me, but I can see that they're about to cry. My father shushes me when I ask what is wrong, and no one tells me why.

The Ending No One Ever Explained

Aafiya doesn't come over
to play any more.

I ask for her every day.
But everyone just looks away.

I never see her again.

A Ghost Lives in This House

It hides in the tremor in
my grandmother's hands. Sometimes
I see it coiled up on my grandfather's tongue
before his usually clear words falter.

It taps through the television screen
when the news speaks of our land.
Bad things happened here,
I am five and I already know it.

We are a soft but strong people
and perhaps that makes us easier to haunt.
We try so hard to wear happiness easily,
even if it is only for each other's eyes.

Try so hard to turn the shadows
into lighter burdens to bear.
No one wants their loved ones
to carry this heavy apparition.

This sword over our necks,
this unnamed reverberation.
The lingering question:
'What remains of a family
                    after partition?'

When We Leave Kashmir

I am six and no one explains why.
To each other they whisper
and I catch words with the eagle ears
I have inherited from my dadi.

Partition. Fresh start. Delhi.
Hushed to the point of murmur.
Independence. Break. Home.
Spoken even softer than a mutter.

The drive is long in the old white Fiat.
Tired of watching the road disappear
and time inching along, I ask my mother,
'Mama, what is partition?'

My mother takes a sharp breath.
My father clears his throat gently.
It takes her a long time to speak.
The words tumble out,

as though they make it hard
for her to breathe.
'It was a terrible time, jaan.
The country was split into parts.

One part is where we live, India.
The other became its own country, Pakistan.
Many people from both countries died.
In our family too.'

Death still did not make sense to me
even though I was raised alongside it.
'Like who?' I asked, pushing my luck
as my rebellious streak grew.

'Your dadi lost two brothers.
Your nani lost three sisters and a brother.'
I did not know what siblings were,
so I pushed a little harder this time.

'But how do you split a country?'
My mother turned back
and looked me carefully in the eye.
'I will tell you when you are older.'

I fall back against the warm leather seat,
defeated, my mouth in a small frown.
'How about, instead,' Mama says soothingly,
'I tell you the story of how the world came to be.'

How the World Came to Be: Mama's Version

In the beginning, there was nothing.

And then love was born.

The first form of love was the Goddess. Like love always is, we could not see her, but simply feel that she was there.

We will call her the Devi, the self, the eternal. She is the mother to the universe, and everything that comes next. Her fingers are the ones that craft the ornate golden egg which holds everything we know.

With her warmth and kindness, the egg bursts open, and the creator Lord Vishnu is born, as fully formed and perfect as his mother imagined him. Dark-haired, four-armed, gentle-faced Vishnu, with a garland of jasmines around his neck, a golden crown on his head. It is Vishnu who creates the four-headed Lord Brahma within a lotus.

Brahma, new to this strange cosmos, and wondering who he is, the way we all do from the moment we are born, decides to paint his dreams awake. He uses the petals of the lotus of his birth to create the sky, the ground, the water. He creates the Gods themselves, who we will call the Devas, and their cousins the Asuras. The stars and the planets and the moon and finally, our own mother Earth.

But still, it is incomplete. You see, there can be no life without death.

For balance to exist, both light and dark must too. All we experience is in cycles, Paro.

Remember that. Even the Earth and the universe we live in is part of a cycle.

This is where the Lord Shiv, the destroyer, slowly reveals his presence. Blue-skinned Shiv, with the snake coiled around his neck, the moon in his hair, who has already destroyed the universe before and will do so again, when the dark imbalances the light. When all beings become more cruel than kind. When the universe needs to be reborn again.

The Devi smiles at the three Gods, our Trimurti, and says, 'Go forth. Create. Destroy. Above all else, make sure truth and the spirit prevails.'

On the Way to Delhi, We Stop at Nani's House

One day somewhere in the future,
someone with gentle eyes will ask me,
'What does paradise look like to you?'

And I will say,
without skipping a beat,
'My grandmother's house.'

I suppose I should admit I am fortunate.
People go their whole lives seeking paradise
and I've had it since I was born.

A home, less home than it is God's own palace.
A garden, less garden and more cosmos.
More universe.

If there was a mouth to heaven,
surely
this would be it.

Not because it is big, for it is small.
Not because it is full of material riches,
but because it is bursting with love.

My grandmother opens her heart to people.
This is why paradise lives here.
In a quiet little house hidden behind lychee trees.

One would almost forget until you hear gunshots
that this is only 10 kilometres from the border,
a source of my mother's constant worry.

And maybe paradise looks different to you,
but for me it is here, and it is this.
My nani's arms

are where my peace lives.
If there was a mouth to heaven,
surely this would be it.

Nani's Lullabies

She calls me Raja Beta,
and Dil Ki Tukdi
and Delight.
There is a fourth name,
but we always forget.

Every night,
before I sleep,
she sings to me about
Chanda Mama,
and Machli Jal Ki Rani.

She tells me one day
I will tire of them,
but I cannot imagine
ever being too old
to hear her lullabies.

Grandmothers are a gift
not to be taken lightly.
So many lose them,
before they are old enough
to know their magic.

I am glad my bones
were born with this knowledge.
She taught me
how to become
a good ancestor.

At least this –
loving her presence,
appreciating her wisdom –
is something
I know how to do well.

Tonight's Tale from Nani

My father's father grew forests.
With his bare hands he nurtured
the earth as he planted
sapling after sapling.

People said that the Goddess Aranyani
guided his hands, Goddess of forests
and deer and rabbits and wolves
and all things wild and free.

He said she spoke to him
through tree bark,
whispering wisdom
to him through his fingers.

'People are trees,'
he used to say.

'They are not,'
my father would disagree,

'because trees stay.'

But they both agreed,
standing in a forest Bade Papa
planted all by himself, that
forests are families.

As long
as the canopy
remains unbroken,
every tree is protected.

As long
as the roots
grow deep into the earth
and entwine with each other

like they are holding hands,
they will remain,
in some form, some shape,
even if they are cut down and broken.

You cannot destroy a family.
Even if you try.
Even through war.
Some part of them always remains.

How to Leave Paradise

Don't.

Hide in God's own room.
Hold your grandmother
and refuse to let her go.
Shut your eyes and pray.
Call the Devi herself.
Tell heaven you want to stay
just for one more day.
Scream as your father
carries you away.

As you watch paradise
grow smaller with each mile
they put between you
and your grandmother,

weep
and weep
and weep.

But remember. Paradise
never made you any promises
it had to keep.

Delhi

Is not Kashmir. Not even close.
Everyone runs here and nothing ever stops.
Mama holds my hand much tighter.

Papa's eyes seem a little warier.
No one tells me what to expect
so I learn to navigate the city by smells.

Marigold and rose scents
mean we are crossing phool bazaar.
Turmeric and red chilli

we must have reached the spice market.
The waft of potatoes being deep-fried
and mint chutney means

street sellers are close by
and we may stop
for golgappas and papdi chaat.

Sweet smells of condensed milk
and masala mean
a chaiwalla is about.

All of this is to say,
when you are little enough
and a city is not your home,

you can learn to make it one anyway.
You just learn to love the smells
of a different place.

Some people say this is where
hope comes to die. Later, I learn,
this is also the city where dreams come alive.

Home

Is a big word for a person as small as me.
Once upon a time home meant Kashmir.
Now home has changed and become Delhi.

I practise the word on the floor in my room.
Home. Draw it in red crayon. Home.
What is the difference, I wonder,

between a house and a home?
Mama explains, 'Home is where
God lives.'

Papa says, 'Home is where
your family and love lives.'
This apartment that smells of paint

doesn't feel godly or loving.
Yet every morning, Mama
still awakens and goes to the temple,

brings home sweet prasad offerings to eat.
And Papa still reads the newspaper
eating rusks and drinking chai.

So perhaps home is simply
familiarity, not family.
Home is where comfort lives,

where eventually the walls
begin to feel like a warm embrace
instead of a cold, strange place.

The Playground

I don't know how isolated I have been
until I meet other children.

And I don't meet them
until I go to my first playground.

The only playmate I ever had was Aafiya
and it's hard to remember her without a sharp pain.

Back in Kashmir, we didn't go out much
due to curfews and bomb scares.

Too many memories of places
that have met death more than they have met children.

I do know that Mama is as excited as I am
because she knows already what I don't.

To swing freely without fear means liberty
without constant pressing anxiety.

The park is small and crowded with children
and the ancient swings creak and groan.

But I do not see it that way.
I see Narnia, I see a fairytale land.

My breath catches in my chest,
I can hear their joy and it calls to me.

I look up at Mama, and her smile
tells me to go be whatever I want to be.

'At least for a little while, Paro.
Be free.'

Papa

Papa is different from most men.
He is generous towards
anyone in need
without thinking.

Once, I saw him give
his favourite sweater
to a child begging
under a streetlight in winter.

Once, I saw him give
all the money in his wallet
to a poor man hoping
to feed his children.

Papa is not like Nana Papa or Dada.
They can be thunder and fury
for no reason at all,
even a word can turn them sour.

No one is scared of Papa.
Not even when he gets angry.
But he never really gets angry,
only sad sometimes when he has to leave.

And that, I feel, is worse.
Because he grows quiet
as a midnight
in a sleeping house.

I know how to handle noise
better than I can handle silence.
So I try hard to make him laugh,
to keep him smiling for house.

Papa says,
'Be who you want to be.
Say what you want to say.
Do not let others steal your voice.'

Papa teaches me early:
'This world is not kind,
that is why you must be brave.
Show it the kindness you wish to see.'

The Sailor

The thing is
he has to go.
He has to
because

How Else Will We Eat
and
Delhi Is Expensive
and

One Day When I'm
Old Enough,
I Will
Understand.

His job is on the sea.
Mama shows me
picture books of big ships
and explains,

'Your father
is the captain,
which means
he runs the whole ship.'

And I touch the page,
thinking, *'At least I know*
what takes him away.
At least I know what to hate.'

Nights are spent sobbing
every time he leaves,
knowing that for months after that
it will be just Mama and me.

I practise the word HOME
in my notebooks again.
It feels less familiar,
more empty.

Baats

'Coming to Delhi is expensive,' Mama explains to me.
'This is why we have to be careful with money, okay?'

I nod sagely, understanding. Where at Dada and Dadi's house,
there is a big kitchen, large airy rooms and two storeys,

this place is small and cramped; but that is okay.
Mama and I have each other. At night she reads me stories.

I know the whole Panchatantra by heart, AND Malgudi Days,
but my favourite thing Mama tells me are baats.

Baats are what we call stories from Mama's childhood,
when she grew up with her little brother, all over India.

Nana Papa was in the army, so they were transferred
from Darjeeling in the hills down to Ooty, Wellington.

Mama would talk about how they never had a lot,
but it was enough to buy a book sometimes.

She would read sitting under lychee trees in their garden,
cool shade from the bristling Indian sun;

everything Mama says sounds like heaven somehow.
Perhaps this is because she is Nani's daughter.

Or perhaps this is how all small children see their mothers.
I think to myself, maybe, just maybe Delhi isn't so bad.

The Fruit Seller

No one teaches you
how to live with something
a bad person does to you.

They just say *don't talk to strangers.*
They just say *good touch and bad touch.*
Maybe it was my fault for being too friendly.

Maybe I am just too used to people
who would die to protect me.
It happened so fast,

this swift and brutal thing.
Mama was buying vegetables
and she let my hand go for a minute.

The bazaar was so busy,
no one saw it happen.
One minute I was by her side

and the next minute someone grabbed me.
I don't remember much
of the next fifteen minutes.

I remember wanting to scream
and a hand closing over my mouth
while another lifted my dress.

I remember his laughter,
laughter that mixed with my tears
and I remember my fear.

I was only seven.
Too young to understand
what happened to me.

All I know is
for years and years
I flinched at touch.

Even the thought
of fruit and bazaars
made me violently ill.

All I know is that my body
was suddenly a secret
to be ashamed of,

a story I told myself
in the dark that no one else
could ever know.

I Don't Mean to Be Difficult

But I am.
I throw tantrums.
I cry all the time.

A sadness has
taken my soulbones
hostage.

I miss Papa and Nani.
I shout at Mama
till she cannot look at me.

I am a storm-skinned child.
I cannot hold back
all the wild temper inside me.

I wish we were in Kashmir
and Papa didn't have to leave.
This is such a lonely city.

Mama never lets me out
of her sight. She says
someone might steal me.

But, Mama, don't you see?
Someone
has already stolen me.

I feel suffocated.
I think, we left the aftermath of war in Kashmir
only to live through a new one in Delhi.

I stop eating.
I stop drawing.
I stop caring.

Mama takes me
to the doctor, but
he says dismissively,

'Little girls are supposed
to be resilient.
She'll calm down eventually.'

What Do Little Girls Dream Of?

Horses and heroines.
Meadows and mandirs.
Songs and sadnesses.
Lullabies and longing.
Apsaras and Asuras.
Ships and swimming.
Flying and falling.
Skies and storms.
Rainbows and running.
Love in all its forms.
Mothers who understand.
Fathers who do not leave.
Hands that do not harm.
Valleys and veils.
Mountains and merriment.
Hurt and heartache.
War and wilting.
Weapons and wolves.
Worlds and wounds.
Pain and panic.
Shame and secrets.
Dances and dresses.
Hope and heaven.
Grandmothers and Goddesses.

Everything except peace.

The Second Visit

I haven't thought about her in years.
Still, I know she is coming
when the wind chimes jingle,
when the moon winks at me,
when I can actually see stars smile
from my bedroom window
when the air smells different,
like the jasmines Mama freezes
in bowls to let melt in the Delhi heat.

And there at midnight she appears
a different form, still Goddess
but more human after all.
Bright eyes of a fairytale,
sapphires around her dark throat,
a mother's smile across her lips,
pale blue saree with borders of gold.
The scent of roses and summer fills the air.

If I was not awake before,
I am now, as she sits gracefully
on the edge of my bed.

'Who are you?' I ask.
She raises her finger to her lips and says,

'I am a part of the Goddess,
and the Goddess is a part of me.
My name is Draupadi.
Now, dear child, let me tell you the second story.'

The Second Story

Many years ago, when the world was a tapestry sewn by simpler people, kings used to send their sons to ashrams to learn the art of warfare, enlightenment, humility, mathematics and science. Their teachers were sages renowned for these virtues, and often, the sons of wealthy kings would study with the sons of humble sages.

So it was that the young Prince Drupada became friends with Drona, the son of his teacher, Rishi Bhardwaja. The two grew so close that Drupada promised Drona that he would share half his kingdom with him. Children, you see, are uncorrupted by wealth and caste, and have a purity in them that the world seizes as they grow up. This was before Drupada became a king. Before his immense wealth turned him from a young, earnest prince into a selfish, cautious king. So when the time came for Drupada to keep his promise to Drona, corruption had grown like a seed inside his once pure heart. He sneered at his old friend who stood in rags with his family, called him a beggar, and had him thrown out of his kingdom.

So many stories begin with love that has curdled until it is hatred. Remember this as you grow.

Drona was not a sage to be slighted. He vowed revenge, and to do so, he started his own ashram. There, the princes of the neighbouring kingdoms came under his tutelage, and he taught them the art of warfare till they were all fearsome warriors. The princes known as the five Pandavas of Hastinapur and the hundred Kauravas of Kuru were cousins and for a long time, they loved each other the way brothers do. Sadly, old grudges have ways of tainting all friendships. At the end of their training, Drona asked for his fee, his gurudakshina, from the young warrior princes who stood before him.

Capture King Drupada and bring him before me in chains.

First, it was the turn of the Kaurava princes, but Drupada's army was large and his generals wily, so they were defeated and returned shamefaced.

Then the five Pandava brothers, led by the fearsome archer Arjun, defeated Drupada and brought him before Drona, in chains and utterly humiliated.

The Kaurava princes watched, glowering, as their younger cousins rejoiced in their victory. Jealousy is wily. Once it wedges its green claws into your heart, it poisons every memory you have.

Drona took half of Drupada's kingdom and released him. But the humiliation of proud men is the fuel that fires a thousand battles and Drupada was consumed by revenge.

Drupada gathered all his advisors and his sages in his half of the kingdom together and performed a series of sacrifices and prayers that would get a son to avenge him. The fires devoured sacrifice after sacrifice and the sages' prayers intensified until …

… I was born.

Imagine my king father's displeasure when the fire first yielded me. A girl. The first face I ever saw was my father's, and his mouth was twisted with sadness. I was already a disappointment. Evidence of his greatest failing.

His eyes remained downcast even when a heavenly voice from the fire told him, 'This girl will bring a great change in the future of dharma, of this kingdom and all the kingdoms in this land.'

But the first mortal words in my defence were spoken by his advisor. 'Do not worry, your majesty. A girl can make a good marriage at least.'

At least. They called me Draupadi to pacify my father Drupada. But they named me *At Least*.

As if I was not the reason behind the greatest war of all. As if my power did not make cities crumble. As if the sages who write the greatest epic of our mythology do not write my name first, before the brother that followed me through the fire. As if women were less dangerous than men – when with a flick of our hair or a twist of our tongues, we can destroy kingdoms.

Never forget that.

We can end kingdoms.

An Interruption

Paro: I have a question.

Draupadi: I am sure you have a thousand. If you let me finish the story, perhaps you will understand.

Paro: But—

Draupadi: Stories are powerful, life-changing events, child. But only if you heed them carefully so you can learn all their lessons.

Paro: Oh.

Draupadi: Should I continue?

Paro: Can I ask questions after?

Draupadi: If you listen well enough, you may not have any questions at all.

The Second Story Continues

My father did get his son. My twin brother followed me through the flames.

As time wore on, we were raised to meet our destinies without ever questioning our father. But within me, the divine fire burned longer than it should have.

Women and fire have much in common. Once a flame catches on, it is impossible to destroy it completely. Even when the fire is ashes, some embers remain.

And sometimes,
those embers become fires
again.

When my father decided it was time for me to marry, no one could predict what would happen next.

The palace was prepared for an ancient ceremony called a sway-amvar. Here, kings and princes from a hundred different kingdoms would compete in a series of tasks set by my father to prove themselves worthy of my hand.

My father chose one task. But he made it one of the most difficult tasks of all. From the high emerald-encrusted ceiling of the gilded great hall where the ceremony was to be conducted, a fish made of pure gold was handcrafted and suspended. Each suitor would have a chance to string a bow and then pierce the eye of the golden fish – by only looking at its reflection within a barrel of water.

Prince after prince failed. Every king fumbled and acted in un-royal ways. Once-close friends suddenly became enemies. Some nearly broke the bow in a temper, others walked away dejected. They will tell you all this was because they coveted me so due to my beauty, but it was not. It was because men who are used to power do not know how to be gracious losers. I watched, a lonely, helpless observer in the making of my own destiny. An object to be won or lost. This is what you must remember, child: no woman is an object, even when they treat her as one. We belong to ourselves; our fate is a destination mapped by our hands. Not fathers or husbands or men at all.

It took a man wearing simple muslin to win my hand amongst all those princes draped in colourful silks and vibrant jewels.

He made it look simple. Strung the bow one-handed, the arrow sliding easy as butter, a single shot – and the fish clattered to the floor, at my feet.

I lifted it, for all to see, the arrow protruding from the ruby eye of the fish. My soon-to-be husband smiled at me, and I felt my heart leap, even as the whole court erupted with fury.

What happened next was predictable and boring, so I will not trouble you with it. As you know by now, kings do not cope well with humiliation and are itching to start wars for any reason. They spill blood the way others spill water. Regardless, what matters is, my husband was not alone. He brought his brothers with him. And because he was the fearsome Arjuna and they, the famous Pandava brothers, he won.

He always won.

Well. *Almost* always.

Another Interruption

Paro: But weren't all the Pandavas your husbands?

Draupadi: You are such an inquisitive child. She will be pleased.

Paro: They tell us stories in the mandir, my mama takes me there on Tuesday mornings sometimes.

Draupadi: It is true. All five brothers became my husbands. It was a simple slip of the tongue that caused this. When the brothers brought me home, the twins, who were the youngest, shouted to their mother, 'Mother, look what Arjuna has won!' And their mother, who had not yet opened the door and seen me, said, 'Share it among yourselves equally.'

Paro: And … that made them all your husbands?

Draupadi: Yes.

Paro: Why?

Draupadi: I lived and loved in a time when it was sacrilege to disobey your mother. People did not know then that disobeying your parents could sometimes craft you a better destiny.

Paro: Do you ever wish—

Draupadi: No. Now, for the end of the tale. Pay attention. This has the lesson you must keep close to your chest as you grow.

The Second Story (The Ending)

The only time Arjuna truly lost was when he let Yudhishthira, the oldest of the brothers, and therefore the emperor, gamble our whole empire away to their cousins, the Kaurava princes.

The Kauravas had never quite forgiven their cousins for being better than them. Whether it came to war or ruling a kingdom, the five Pandava brothers excelled. This is why even though the Pandavas and the Kauravas should have ruled the land of Varnavrat together with the help of the God Krishna, the jealous cousins gave us the desert of Khandavprastha to rule instead. My five husbands, never daunted by any hardship that came their way, built the wasteland they had inherited into the beautiful kingdom of Indraprastha.

The shining glory was my palace of illusions. Many do not know this, but I was raised to know finances. In my father's kingdom, advisors came to me with problems within the treasury. Here, in our empire, I became the empress who ran our treasury and knew our citizens by name. There is no point in ruling over a people if you do not know who the people are. If you do not walk in their shoes. The Goddesses, the Gods and their constant reincarnations have taught us this.

For a time, everything was good.

But grudges that have been festering for years and nurtured through jealousy are powerful things. And so it was that the Kaurava princes decided they wanted Indraprastha for themselves.

Yudhishthira was wise. But even the wisest and the kindest of us have our vices. For Yudhishthira, it was gambling. The Kaurava princes knew this. So they organised what they called a friendly game of dice and invited their cousins to come and play. In the end it was just Yudhishthira and Duryodhana left. And Duryodhana was excellent at dice.

So Yudhishthira gambled away his fine horses, his fields, his lands, his palace, his people, his brothers, and, finally, when he had nothing left to gamble, he gambled me. I protested this till my throat was parched and sore, but the courtiers sneered and said women could not question men. Not even when they were empresses.

And as Arjuna and my other husbands watched, Yudhishthira lost me to the most hateful of the Kaurava princes, Duryodhana.

Duryodhana was the one who stoked the fires of jealousy the most among his brothers. He was the engineer behind this game and had his reasons for wanting to humiliate me. Once, a long time ago, I had laughed at him for his foolishness when he fell for an illusion at my palace. He had nursed that slight for years.

His eyes glittered with malice as he sent his brother to fetch me. I was grasped by my hair and dragged out in front of the court.

The shock at this violence rendered me speechless for a few minutes. I looked to my husbands for help but they averted their eyes. Were they simply going to watch as Duryodhana insulted me?

The answer was yes.

I begged. I pleaded with the elders in the court. Duryodhana's cruel laughter echoed through the palace as I wept. When they come for our bodies, child, nothing their hands can do will ever compete with the sheer evil of their laughter as they do it.

They did their best to humiliate me. Tried to undress me in front of hundreds of men. Tried to make me sit on the knees of lecherous Kaurava princes. And while my husbands did not help, the Gods and Goddesses did.

I grew stronger than a hundred men and fought them off my body. When they grasped my saree to pull it off, I prayed to my brother, the Lord Krishna, and the saree's fabric grew so long they could not succeed and fell exhausted at my feet.

When they finally let us go into exile, unable to steal my dignity from me, I told my husbands that I would never, ever forgive them for abandoning me in my hour of need.

I told them that it would take a war to win back my favour. That I would not wash my hair until it was soaked in the blood of the men who assaulted me. That I would not rest until I watched every Kaurava turned to ash and bone. This rage was my gift, my blessing, and I would use it to bring my enemies to their knees. I would be the fuel my husbands needed.

There is a reason some reincarnated me into Kritya, wicked woman. Rakshasi the monster woman. The spark that lit one of the greatest wars of antiquity, the Mahabharata.

But after hearing what I have endured, can you blame me?

What I Learned from Draupadi

Rage is an ancient gift,
passed down from Goddess to woman,

but wielding it well
is a talent few are given.

If I do not control it,
it will come at the cost of everyone I love,

but to learn to carry it with grace,
will only be once I tame my own fire's roar.

Phone Calls

The third time
I make Mama cry,
she calls Nani.

We have an old black telephone
that sits on the glass-top wicker table
by the balcony,

and a soft purple chair
with wooden legs
where Mama sits, receiver in hand.

She tells Nani,
'I don't know
what's wrong with her.'

And,
'Something is changed,
and I don't know how to fix it.'

And,
'Was I ever
this difficult?'

But the truth is,
I am a much more difficult child
than my mother ever was.

Nani so often tells Mama,
'You're the best daughter
a parent could ask for.'

Mama talks for a while more,
and then calls me close
and hands the receiver to me.

I hold the cold plastic
to my ear
and say, 'Hello?'

'Raja Beta,
Dil Ki Tukdi,
what hurts you, my delight?'

And for reasons known only to my heart,
just the sound of her voice
crackling on the other end

of this unclear line
causes a dam to break
open inside my chest.

I sit down heavily
on the icy floor
to cry and cry.

The Airport

We go to get Papa at the airport.
Mama drives us there in the old Fiat,
and on the way, she tells me,

'Paro, when you grow up,
make sure you can drive,
get your own car.'

I look at her:
her hazel eyes focusing
so sharply on the road,

the way her hand
moves so confidently
between the steering wheel

and the gear stick,
never making a mistake,
never panicking, even on a busy road,

and ask, 'Why?'
A smile graces Mama's lips.
'Independence is the greatest treasure.

For a man, yes,
but for a woman
even more so.'

I don't understand
what she means yet.
Before I ask more questions,

she smoothly parks the car
and as we step out
into the sweltering heat,

we see planes rising into
the blue, clear sky,
sunlight glittering off their wings,

growing smaller and smaller
as they fly higher and farther
till we can not see them at all.

'We will go in a plane
one day soon,'
Mama says to me.

The thought makes
my tummy feel funny,
but before I can say anything,

we see Papa wheeling
his trolley out with
his baggage,

the biggest grin
on his bearded face as he shouts,
'MY GIRLS!'

Mama throws her head back and laughs.
I break into a run
as he crouches,

arms wide open to catch me
in the greatest bear hug.
I don't know a whole lot,

but I definitely know
safety is
my father's arms.

Indra

I was seven when Indra was born.
He came out blue, screaming,
the umbilical cord wrapped around his neck.
They had to cut Mama open to get him.

Your mama was so brave,
they tell me.
He nearly died,
they tell me.

I knew from that moment on
he was trouble.
I also knew that I would do anything
to protect him.

To be an older sister is to know
you will be asked to be your sibling's mother.
That you now have responsibilities.
That as you count his ten fingers

and ten little toes, you know
he needs you to be the best
of not only who you are,
but who you wish to be.

After Indra Was Born

Mama and he came home,
everyone said how handsome he was.

And how he looked just like my father.
And how Mama must be so happy

now that they had a son.
And Mama changed too.

I was still her firstborn,
but not her only priority any more.

'You're older, Paro.
You can manage.'

I heard that a lot.
I learned later girls heard that a lot.

I discovered this as I watched
my baby brother grow up

being allowed to be a child
for as long as he needed to be.

But ever since I was little,
I knew how to make paranthas,

how to change my brother's diapers,
how to carry him and sing him to sleep,

how to lock the house,
how to make masala chai,

how to keep our home clean.
My parents smiled and said,

'What a good mother you are already,'
and, really, I didn't mind.

I liked helping Mama so I beamed.
But still at night, when I slept,

I dreamed of a different world –
one where I was allowed

to be a child
as long as I needed to be.

The Crib

Indra sleeps in Mama-Papa's room.
He has a soft, cloth crib in a corner.
It's the same grey as a stormy day
and filled with Indra's favourite toys.
Elephant and eagle soft toys,
because even as a baby,
these are his favourite two animals.

I go to look at him often.
He's so tiny. No bigger than his toys.
I ask Mama, 'Was I so little once?'
She drops a kiss on top of my head
as she pulls Indra out to feed him.
'Yes. You were so small, we could
hold you in one hand.'

I think about that. It fascinates me.
Whose hand? Mama and Papa's?
Would Indra fit into my hand?
The thought lodges itself inside my head.
I can't get rid of it no matter what I do.
One day when he is sleeping,
I decide to find out.

While Mama is asleep, I carefully tiptoe in.
Gently, I reach into the crib,
my small arms wavering,
and I lift Indra up with both hands
as I've seen Mama do.
I am not allowed to do this without Mama watching me.
He gurgles, his just-opened black eyes shining,
reaching to tug my hair.

'Paro!'

A voice behind startles me.
My fingers slip before I know what is happening
and Indra falls to the ground.
Mama shrieks and runs towards us from the bed
as Indra's cries erupt across the room.
I try to pick him up, but she pushes me away.
'GO TO YOUR ROOM NOW!'

I learn that day
how awful regret can taste
when it wears the skin
of your own mistakes,
and you cannot look away;
all you have is your own discomfort
and no one else to blame.

First Day of School

Someone tells Mama
this is the cure
for unruly children.

School is good
because it keeps us preoccupied,
gives us something to do.

The first thing I see is terrified faces.
Everyone here is as scared as me.
At least in that there is some unity.

I think I am being punished.
For being difficult, for not listening.
I look up at Mama pleadingly,

I'll be good, I promise.
Don't send me away,
I try to tell her with my eyes.

Mama just holds my hand tighter
as all mamas are prone to do,
I've discovered.

The room is small
and clammy with sweat
and the smell of Plasticine.

A tall lady in a salwar kameez
of gold and green says,
'Come, Paro.'

She reaches for my hand,
and I feel Mama hold on
for a second, unable to let go.

When she does,
fear clamps
down on my throat.

Mama sees the fear
and says, 'Paro, don't worry.
I'll be here when you're done.

Now go on,
go join the other children.
Have some fun.'

Childhood's End

It happens suddenly.
One day, your parents
don't pick you up any more.
Responsibilities grow.
Your mother starts focusing
on other things.
Maybe a job or a sibling.
You grow a bit quieter.
Maybe it's because of
A Thing That Happened To You.
Whatever the reason may be,
one day, you are small,
and hold a world of games
inside your chest.
And the next,
suddenly none
of the games
make any sense.

Kishoravastha

Teenage

You will learn slowly,
that your greatest masterpiece
is not the act of survival.

It is how to craft graciousness
in the face of outgrowing
what you thought you needed to survive.

Twelve

This is what the cliff-edge of girlhood looks like:

You still drink ice-cold milk with Rooh Afza in it, but masala chai is starting to grow on you. You're beginning to forget Kashmir so you watch old family VHS tapes with your mother hoping everything remains vibrant in your mind. Slowly things fade. You're scared you'll forget your nani's house and your childhood. Don't fret. You'll learn later that the memory is just in the habit of turning itself into an oil painting. Your wrists are still little enough to break, but your chest is growing bigger. You haven't had your period but you know it is coming and you're scared. You don't know what to do with your fear; you just know when it does come, it has to be a secret you keep to yourself. When your mother gives you your first pads, she will bring the packet hidden in newspaper. No one will tell you why the blood you lose monthly from your womb is different from the blood you lose from your fingers – why only one of them is a matter of shame. Delhi is still Delhi, all vibrant colours and heat and dust, but the word 'home' will catch on your tongue when you talk about it. You've grown into your body awkwardly and people have started to look at you differently. You don't know what to do with that other than wear baggier T-shirts when you go out to play. The boys won't let you play cricket with them any more and they won't tell you why, but a part of you doesn't really want to play with them either. The girls sit away from the boys and talk about them – first crushes are already blooming. You join them often but you're not sure if you fit in with them either. You try anyway. Mama makes you trade your shorts for jeans. Even in the summer. It's because you're so tall and people stare at your legs all the time, she says, so you have to choose between freedom and comfort. You choose freedom. Of course you choose freedom. Your mother is still the person you go to for everything, whether wound or joy. One day this will stop. Not yet. Your father is mostly absent so you can eat and go to school and have shelter. One day this will hit you hard, how much he has given up for you. Not yet. Your brother is small and still looks up to you. One day, he will tower over you. Not yet. You can walk to the shops on your own now, but you avoid crowds and bazaars. You will try to do that for ever. You won't always succeed. You still have nightmares about what happened to you when you were seven. You don't like hugging anyone who isn't your immediate family and tremble when relatives try to hug you whether you like it or not. No one asks why. Your mother notices and sometimes rescues you, but sometimes tells you to behave yourself. Your body feels like it doesn't belong to you. You don't know anything about love. This will change and you will fall so hard, the time you broke your leg when you were eight will feel like a walk in the park. One day, you will stop drinking milk with Rooh Afza in it. Your drink of choice will become masala chai instead.

Not yet, though.

Not yet.

Six Years in Delhi

I go to Big School now,
and Mama tells her friends,

'She's doing so much better.'
And yes, she's probably right.

Being a big sister changes you.
You learn How To Be Responsible.

And How To Put Others First
Even If You Don't Want To.

But not How To Stop Nightmares
About Bazaars and Brutality.

None of these are lessons
they teach in school.

In school we learn civics
and geography and science

and maths, which I absolutely hate.
But I love English and art

and zero period because of Mrs Agnihotri,
our class teacher but also my favourite teacher.

But the scariest lesson for me is history,
because it makes me so angry.

What We Learn in History Class

India was once Sone ki Chidiya,
a golden bird that flew and sang free,
her bejewelled feathers were her provinces,
ruled by a thousand different kings and queens.

But when you glow so bright
that even the Sun God Surya
cannot help but cover his eyes,
you attract dangerous attention.

When the men arrived
to claim her for themselves,
they did it through violence
and exploitation.

But even when they stole her feathers
and caged her in the dark,
they could not dull her shine,
her songs, nor take her soul's freedom.

There is a reason we call India, *she.*
Her road to freedom was as hard-won,
as furious as any survivor's is destined to be;
and women are the fiercest survivors I know.

What We Learn in History Class (2)

My country used to be a colony.
'This means,' Mrs Krishnan says,
'that the British came to India,
and decided they would keep it for themselves.'

'But, Mrs Krishnan,' I raise my hand and ask,
'what about the people who lived here already?'
My teacher, the tallest woman I have ever met,
voted by every student as the strictest in school,

lets a shadow of a smile sit on her lips.
'This is a good question.
For homework write about what happened
to the people of the country the British colonised.'

My classmates may have sighed
and been annoyed with me,
but when I return home to show Mama the assignment,
she reads it carefully

then chooses books from her shelf
and hands them to me.
She says, 'This is a powerful lesson
and one you must learn yourself.'

What Happened to the People the British Colonised

A History Poem by Paro Madera

We were told to learn a language
and place it before our mother tongues.

We were told to pray to a new, paler God
over the millions that were known to us.

We were told this would save us,
but we already knew how to save ourselves.

It's not what we HAD to do,
but it was 'what was expected'.

And by that they meant,
'It is urgent that you assimilate.'

And by *assimilate*, they meant,
'Become like us or our guns will take care of the rest.'

But they will never see us like them.
Our skin is too brown,

our eyes too onyx and earthen,
our religions too beautifully unusual,

and our Goddesses too powerful
for their comfort.

So instead they turn us against each other.
Use kingdom against kingdom.

Stoke and nurture hatreds within us
to help them erase our culture.

Mrs Krishnan's Comments

Marks: 5/10

This is not the assignment I asked for. Rewrite as an essay and expand on the sociopolitical implications of British Raj on the people of India and Pakistan. Build on the fact that India's GDP did not grow under the British Raj due to their imperial policy. In today's terms, trillions were taken in resources from Indo-Pak to Britain. Hand in on Monday morning.

I enjoyed your poem. Keep writing.

'When I Was Four ...'

begins Indra, now at the ripe old age of six,
his shorts so large they balloon around his little legs.

After school, we both sit with our faces on our hands,
cross-legged on Mama's bed as we talk about our days.

'When I was FOUR,' Indra repeats, annoyed as his lisp
gets in the way of his words, making his F sound like P,

'we went to a BIG ship and Papa was captain,
and then we sailed and sailed till we reached Mad – Mad—'

'Madagascar,' I grin, one of my front teeth still missing.
He nods, takes a deep breath again and says,

'We went THERE and everyone was really nice
and a big blue bird sat on my shoulder.'

My little brother is all huge eyes, a ski-jump nose
and long meandering stories.

He is both my favourite human in the world,
and the most annoying person I know.

Every summer, we join my father on his ship
to travel across the sea to faraway lands.

I know one day this will stop. We will be too old
to join my father at sea. My brother will grow quieter

the way Shalini's brother Karan has been since he turned nine.
Still, as we practise our daily after-school ritual of storytelling,

and Indra chatters on about ships and trees and blue birds,
a part of me wishes he would never ever grow up.

Shalini's House

In the evenings now,
I don't really go out to play.
The playground belongs
to children Indra's age.

And while he enjoys the swings
and screams down the slides,
the way I used to in a memory
not too far gone,

Mama takes me to Shalini's house.
Our mothers are friends,
and usually that means
we should be close too.

Shalini greets Mama warmly,
and says, 'Hi, Auntie,
so lovely to see you
and Paro here.'

While Mama and Sunita Auntie talk,
Shalini and I are sent to her room.
But Shalini doesn't like me.
She has made that clear.

'We live in a big house,
and you live in a little apartment,'
she said the first time we met.
'We are not like you.'

And by this she means,
'My family has more money
than yours ever will,
and this makes us better than you.'

And by this she means,
'I'll be nice to you
for our mothers' sakes,
but I am not your friend.'

It seems strange to me
that coin
and paper
get to decide the value of a person.

The same way it felt strange
when my dadi told me,
'We are not like them,'
about Aafiya and her family.

But as Shalini picks up a comic to ignore me
in her room of lime green and pale pink
with a brand new computer
and a sputtering air conditioner and TV,

I look at the photographs on the table
and notice how distant
her father looks and how sad
she and her brother look in all three.

'Mama, Are We Poor?'

The corner of my mother's mouth
turns down slightly.
'Why would you ask that, baby?'

She calls both Indra and I *baby*
when she worries. I look down
at my white, secret, clenching knuckles.

Should I break the unspoken rules
and tell her about how Shalini really is with me?
'I just … Sunita Auntie's house …'

But the words refuse to leave my lips.
My mother doesn't say anything.
I notice that instead of turning the car left,

which is how we get home,
she has taken us right.
'Let me show you something.'

Trucks speed past us on this dusty road
as the car moves uphill past the traffic lights.
Finally, she pulls over to the side and stops the car.

'I'm glad that
it is still daylight
and I can show you this.'

I peek over the windshield
at what she is gesturing at.
'Where are we, Mama?'

The car is parked on a hill
overlooking a small village.
It was patchwork cement-free brick structures,

uneven canvases for makeshift roofs.
Children ran with no clothes on,
some were as old as Indra.

'I want you to remember this,'
Mama's voice cuts in quietly,
'the next time you think we have less.

We are fortunate, Paro. We have food to eat.
A home to come back to.
Your brother and you go to school.

All because you were born into a family
that could afford these things for you.
This is called a privilege and you must never forget it.'

I ponder these words as I watch girls
my own age with torn clothes look after their siblings
in a far more maternal way than I look after Indra.

Shamefaced, I understand what she is teaching me.
'Being aware of it is not about being ashamed, Paro,'
Mama says quietly and I realise my cheeks have turned red.

'It is about using that privilege to help and raise others up.
It is about fighting to create a more equal world.
Would you like to come with me on the weekends

and help teach and feed the children here?'
I look up at her and nod. Mama smiles.
'Good. Now let's go home and prepare for Rakhi.'

When I Was Eight, Nani Explained
Rakhi As …

'The festival of brothers and sisters.
Where sisters tie talismans to their brothers' wrists
and brothers give sisters presents and promise
they will protect them.'

She was making kheer,
which is my favourite,
and I was holding the saffron threads
in my cupped hands like they were treasure.

And I asked,
'But, Nani, what if someone
doesn't have a brother
or a sister?'

She stopped stirring the hot, sweet
rice and milk, and looked at me.
'Do you know
how Rakhsha Bandhan began?'

I shook my head slowly.
Nani wiped her hands
on a towel and gently
took the saffron threads from my hands.

'Many, many years ago,
the Lord Krishna, a reincarnation
of Lord Vishnu, cut his finger
while handling some sugar cane.

Draupadi, wife of the Pandavas,
who was nearby,
ripped a piece of her saree
and bandaged his hand with it.

Lord Krishna, touched,
promised her unending
brotherly protection
and love.

Draupadi was not his sister
through blood, but became
his sister through
kindness and love.

Ever since then,
we celebrate Rakhsha Bandhan.
But we remember that family
is not just those of blood.

But also those
we choose to love.'

What Rakhi Means in My House

I make the talisman myself in school.
Bright red and gold thread twisted together,
a red stone shaped like a tear drop in the centre.

I use red because red is holy.
I use gold, gold for prosperity.
I say an intention of protection,

because it is my job as his big sister
to make sure I can protect him
from everything that might hurt him.

We say a prayer to the Goddesses and Gods first.
And then Mama holds the tray where we have lit
a diya and put the rakhi and some ladoos.

Indra wants to light the incense,
but since he is little I hold his hands
and help him strike the match.

Then, I press a red tikka against his forehead
and tie the rakhi to his little wrist.
He yells and claps his hands, gap-tooth grin showing.

'Red is my favourite!'
Mama holds out a shiny, blue-wrapped square present
to Indra, he holds it like it is treasure and gives it to me.

I open it slowly and with care
It's a sketchbook
and a steel tin of graphite pencils.

I haven't drawn in years,
but Indra's expectant, glowing face
makes me want to again.

[handwritten note: lot's of vibrant colors!]

Damini

She walked 3 miles from her village
when she first came to our house,
and she brought with her blistered feet and the kindest smile.

Mama gave her Dettol,
bandages, my old tennis shoes
and the job she asked for almost instantly.

Mama also never lets her walk again
and goes to pick her up and drop her off
despite Damini telling her not to trouble herself.

We went to the village to help Damini's people.
I help my mother heal, teach and feed people,
but it never feels like we are doing enough to help.

Sometimes Mama sighs. 'I wonder if I am only
really helping myself feel better than helping anyone else.'
And I try really hard to make sense of this.

Damini is only six years older than me.
And until Mama buys her more clothes,
every day she would wear the same faded blue salwar kameez.

Her family is poor
so she doesn't get to go to school
like Indra and me.

She sweeps and swabs and cleans our toilets
so she can help feed her family.
Everyone I know has 'help',

and by 'help' I mean someone else's
daughters, mothers, sisters,
who have no choice but to walk miles

so they can do the jobs no one else wants to
for very little money that will feed their families.
I ask my teachers why life is so unfair to Damini.

Why isn't Damini allowed to go to school like me?
Why does money get to dictate the life she leads?
The adults in my life never give answers that satisfy.

This is just fate, luck, the card game of life.
They must have done something wrong in a previous life.
They just aren't like us. They aren't like us.

But to me, that answer explained little,
but when I asked too many questions close to the truth,
all the grown-ups told me I was being rude.

And neither
does it sound
like the truth.

For the Girl Who Calls Me Didi

If the world could magic itself into a fairer place,
I hope it would become somewhere where girls like Damini

were rewarded
instead of punished.

Damini is one of the cleverest people I know.
She has a quicksilver tongue and can bargain

with any shopkeeper till it suits what is in her pocket.
She is bubbly and smiles all the time,

but if you look at her face closely,
you see the sadness bruise her eyes.

She says eagerly, 'Didi, humko bhi sikhao English.'
Because she wants to learn English.

When I teach her, I am humbled by her determination,
her ability to turn a foreign phrase so perfectly

that it sounds like it always belonged on her lips.
She calls me Didi. Didi means sister.

I wish I had actually done something worthy
to earn and deserve such a tender moniker.

The Wish

In Class Six, for homework,
our class teacher, Mrs Agnihotri,
asked us to write down our biggest wish.

I watched as Mohit and Ram
laughed and made jokes
and no one stopped them,

but the minute Shalini
or I did, we were told,
'Silence, no giggling.'

I learned from Damini that
her father and brother don't work.
Only she and her mother do.

I watched my mother fret
about housework and washing
as my father watched TV.

I think about what Mama said
about privilege and wonder
if men are privileged in a way women are not.

But then I watched as Indra,
only six, was allowed
to go to friends' houses already,

but when I asked to go out,
I was eyed with suspicion
to make sure there was no other ploy.

I looked down at my notebook
that evening and wrote clearly:

I wish I had the freedom of a boy.

Something Shifted After I Wrote Those Words, the Air Changed Forever

The sheet sticks to my skin
as I watch the ceiling fan turn slowly.
Sweat slides from my forehead.
The air is thick with something
I cannot describe.

Sulphur winds its way in
from a window overlooking
the glittering, smoggy city.
And suddenly, without warning,
a windswept Goddess stands before me.

I only know she is a Goddess,
because I remember Draupadi.
But this being is surrounded
by fireflies, a crackling energy,
a giant black cat glides with her gracefully,

and a part of me wants to scream.
But she is golden-skinned, twigs in her hair,
emerald in her nose and soft smiles.
Kajal-rimmed abyss eyes
glittering with hope,

she takes my clammy hand
in her cool one and says gently,
'Let me show you why
you should never wish to be anyone
except who you are already.'

The Third Story

I too have hated my destiny and wished to be anyone else.

I too have carried wounds inside me and let them change who I am into someone angry.

As far as Goddesses go, not many have heard of me. There are no ashrams or books that teach people about me. I exist now through the words of ancient women, who whisper me into their daughters' ears as they are about to give birth, who pray to me for healthy children. Some say I was born a demon, others say I was always a Goddess, but all agree, I am the Goddess of nurture, of children, of soon-to-be mothers.

My name is Shashthi. I was born in a golden forest within a goddess, the child of an Asura queen and Deva. You know by now, child, that Asuras and Devas, though cousins, are sworn enemies. They are not supposed to fall in love and have children. My parents, unable to hide me themselves, begged the great Devi to hide me.

And so she swallowed me whole to keep me safe, and when I was old enough, she gave me permission to leave the forest. She kissed my forehead and told me, 'Shashthi, I cannot keep you hidden away for ever. You have a purpose, as we all do. Go and find what fate intends for you.' She gave me a gift, my companion the black cat, so I would not be lonely, and he and I rode across the stars to this earth.

I knew so little of the universe then. The Asura side of me was reckless and wild. It still held resentment towards the parents who had abandoned me and this, coupled with loneliness, made for a dangerous recipe. I wished from the bottom of my heart to be someone else. Either Asura or Deva, but not both. Never both. So when no one answered my prayers, I grew angry. I took my temper out on new mothers, my anger manifesting in the devouring of children on the sixth day of their birth. I was malicious, bringing suffering with me wherever I went. Fear grew synonymous with my name.

Terrible things happen when you let bitterness rule your bones. One day you look into a mirror and cannot recognise who you are any more.

My mirror came to me too. My vahana, this same black cat, had left me to go and live in the form of a small regular cat in a simple house with seven sons. It could not take the cries of the mothers I punished. Animals come from purer parts of the universe. They are not like us.

The house he went to had seven daughters-in-law and the very youngest one loved food. She stole it often. When she was caught, she would blame the black cat, who would in turn get beaten within an inch of his life. Of course, because he could not speak in human tongues, he was unable to defend himself. Remember, child, it is one of the greatest sins to do this, to blame something or someone who cannot defend themselves.

The banyan trees carried this cruel secret to me and I felt my very blood curdle with fury. Each of my footsteps lit a fire as I reached the house and there, crying in pain, I found my dear black cat. I healed him with neem roots as he told me his tale. Seeing it with my own eyes, my anger grew to rage. While the woman lay sleeping, I stole her firstborn son.

As I was about to devour him, the baby gurgled and opened his eyes, and there, in that moment, something changed within my spirit. Perhaps it was the way he laughed so fearlessly and innocently, or how he reached for one of my necklaces. Instead of devouring him, I chose to raise him as my own. Six times the girl gave birth and all six sons I stole. I justified it by saying, *liars like her do not deserve children.*

This was selfish, and I should have known better. It was through watching the children grow and play that I realised my error.

Never underestimate a mother's love for her children. As I played surrogate mother to six human sons, the Devi in me slowly grew until she burst out of my chest and she and I were one. This was why the broken mother of the boys prayed and prayed until I relented, for motherhood had made me soft in turn. And when I arrived before her, she begged for her children. I made her ask forgiveness from my four-legged companion first. I made her promise she would never again lie and lay blame on an innocent again. She relented, took her children, and then spread this story far and wide till eventually it overshadowed the stories of when I was cruel and bitter. I became known for mercy and mother-hood. I reincarnated into a version of myself I loved better. Do you understand?

This is how I became Shashthi Mata.

From that moment on, I have been different – not the devourer of children, but their protector, not the punisher of mothers, but their guardian.

What I am trying to say is, it is only through exploring your shadow self that you can reach enlightenment.

What I am trying to say is, it is only through accepting the parts that you are ashamed of that you can truly know yourself.

After the Third Visit

Paro: But what if you do not accept those parts of yourself?

Shashthi: Then you will never find your purpose and you will wander through your life full of self-loathing.

Paro: And what if there are things inside you that are much too difficult to love and you wished you were someone else instead?

Shashthi: Then you learn how to read yourself better.

Paro: But what if the world hates you for who you are?

Shashthi: Then you give them a kinder story to tell.

Paro: How did you learn to forgive yourself for all the pain you gave others?

Shashthi: I have not. Forgiveness is easier to give to others than to yourself. But I am slowly learning. Each good deed I do eases some of the evil I once did. Now, sleep. We will see you one day again.

The rain speaks to me as it falls.
The wind chimes sing lullabies.
The smell of sulphur is gone,
and I find myself alone.

Whistling

The day after is a good day.
Monsoon has come early,
quenching the thirst of the dry city.
The sky wears a fresh pink-orange dress.
The smell of petrichor rises
to meet me with each skip.
I am on my way to pick up samosas
so we can have them with chai.

The thought makes my heart swell.
I start whistling to let my bursting happiness out.
The wind picks up and dandelion seeds fly-dance past me.
I almost don't see Mr Singh on his manicured lawn.

Every girl in the colony avoids this route.
But Shashthi has made me braver
so I take the short route past his garden.
His moustache bristles as he sees me and

his bottlenose glasses
make his judging eyes larger
He spits, 'Girls shouldn't whistle.
Didn't your mother teach you manners?'

On a normal day, this would make me crumble.
But as I said, today is a good day.
And I am a wiser version of myself. So I say cheekily,
'My mother taught me plenty, Mr Singh,

but her best lesson is never to listen
when someone tells me what a girl can or cannot do.'
When I skip away in defiance,
I make sure my whistle-song is even louder.
            just to get under his skin.

Mrs Agnihotri

Gives us another kind of assignment.
Write a personal manifesto.

Mrs Agnihotri is always giving us
assignments like that.

She calls it *emotional development.*
She never gives us any marks on them.

She says, 'Marks ruin the point
of assignments like this.'

I don't think the other schoolteachers like her.
Sometimes I hear them in the corridors

saying she's strange, saying she wears colourful
salwar kameez when she should be wearing sober sarees.

They whisper she is *too New Agey*
with her jangly earrings and colourful bangles.

I really like Mrs Agnihotri. All of us do.
Her assignments are the best ones.

I go home and look up MANIFESTO
in the dictionary. It means:

'A public declaration of motives, intentions
or views of the issuer be it an individual or group.'

I think for hours about what Shashthi taught me,
looking out towards the city.

Then I open the red notebook I keep for
Mrs Agnihotri's lessons, and with a black pen
print out carefully:

How To Be a Revolution of a Girl

A Manifesto by Paro Madera

You can be a revolution even when you are only twelve years old. Even when you think you are too small, you can do this:

1. When the boy in your class pulls your hair like it is a rope on the playground and the teacher dismisses it with 'Oh, he must like you', you look her in the eye and say, 'People who like you do not hurt you – and you shouldn't encourage that.'

2. When the school bus driver leers too long at you, turning your body into a feast for his eyes, do not hide yourself away in shame. Instead tell him as you get off the bus that you bet he has a daughter your age and men glare at her the same way.

3. When the boys in class draw all the women teachers on their knees before men on the blackboard, you do not join in with nervous laughter. Ignore their jeers, pick the duster up and erase their misogyny before their eyes.

4. When someone grabs at your chest 'accidentally' in the cafeteria, you slap that hand as hard as you can.

5. When boys pull at your bra straps to let them land on your skin with stinging snaps, do not run. Instead, claw at their hands. Let them know if they lay their hands on you, their hands will come back wounded.

6. Teach your baby brother how to do little things like make his own bed and tidy things away – teach him that these aren't 'girl things'.

7. Be inconvenient. Raise your hand despite their groans. Voice your opinions. Enter debates. Classrooms are not only boys' domains.

8. If they sigh and say, 'Boys will be boys', to justify why boys get to do what you don't, smile sweetly and say, 'And girls will be girls.' Then do what you want anyway.

Thirteen

It will happen at a wedding. In an explosion of jasmine scent and colour-coordinated chaos.

Your mother will make you wear a pale pink lehenga instead of a comfortable salwar kameez this time, and when you tell her the embroidery of stones and beads itches, she will tell you that you are thirteen next week and you must learn that one of the principles of womanhood is learning how to bear pain with grace. You won't understand why you must give up comfort, but you trust her so you imagine you will understand better when you are older. Your brother will cry and complain about how itchy his clothes are till his cheeks are red with fury. Your mother will placate him with the promise of ice cream.

The hotel and the wedding will seem otherworldly. Mauve orchids and white jasmine will decorate a marble staircase leading up to a hall with gold floors, scarlet carpets and chandeliers. Everyone there will look like they have just stepped out of a cinema screen; there will be joy and laughter beyond your wildest dreams. Uncles and aunties you haven't seen for ever will come forwards to hug you and your parents.

Your favourite family friend is getting married. She's only twenty-two. Her mother meets your mother at the entrance, and the first thing she says is, 'They're an industrialist family. The boy has done so well for himself. Thank goodness, I think this will cure all of her wild ways.' And you will wince, but you don't know why. The hall will smell like swarg, the home of the Devas themselves. White tables laden with every kind of roti and naan and dal and murgh makhani and phirni and cake. The family has spared no expense, and as your parents easily mingle and chat with their own friends, you escape to find the bride, your favourite family friend. On the way, you will be caught by older aunties and brought to their table. 'Do you remember me? I last met you when you were so small.' And you won't, but you will nod politely anyway, and they will tell you that you are pretty and you will blush brightly.

As you sit and drink a Fanta they have placed in front of you, the auntie with a bouffant and a tiara will say to the auntie with the mole on her nose in the black and gold saree, 'Now this is a good girl. But did you hear about Jassi's daughter? Such a shame. Only seventeen and has already had an abortion. Destroyed her family's reputation. So much badnaami.' A disquieting discomfort will make your tummy hurt and you will drink your Fanta faster. 'What about Mano's son? He was expelled for bad behaviour, completely ruined his future.' The panic will rise in your throat and the hum of the people around you will feel like a roar. 'And Saloni's girl? I don't know. All these young mothers are just raising their children badly. You would never find any of this in my day.' And you will wonder why fathers aren't blamed when a child makes a mistake. You will excuse yourself because you cannot hear any more, and ask how to find the bride. The groom, a tall man with greying hair in a smart blue achkan, will say, 'She went to her dressing room.'

You will rush to open the door, and almost not see her. She is a swirl of red and gold, bangles and whispering, facing a wall. At least at first you think she is facing a wall. Just as you are about to say her name, you see it. The green of the saree peeks through and you see the henna-covered arms slip around your friend's waist, draw her close. Your ears will hear the sound of the kiss even if your eyes will insist that what you're seeing is not real. You will hear a strangled sob against a mouth. A stolen 'I love you' so soft it could be the whisper of silk against silk. An 'I'm sorry' that sounds more like 'I am drowning'. The girl in green will see you over her shoulder and your friend's tear-stained face will follow her gaze to meet yours.

As her mouth opens to say 'Paro', you will fall back from the door, your mind heavy with things you cannot name and you will walk away, your face hot with confusion.

Later, you will tell your mother about it, simply because you tell her almost everything. Your mother will say, 'That is not true. You must have imagined it.' And when you insist, she will turn to you, hazel eyes blazing with fury, and you will know to drop it. But you know the truth. You *know* what you saw.

Soon, your favourite family friend's name will disappear from everyone's mouths around you. Soon, she will refuse to take your calls and you will be left wondering what you did wrong. Soon, your heart will crack to pieces when you realise hell is loving someone so much you call them your favourite and they want nothing to do with you any more, and you don't even know what you did wrong.

It will happen at a wedding. In an explosion of jasmine scent and colour-coordinated chaos you will learn that being a girl is dangerous to a world that refuses to accept us for who we are.

Mama Says

'Thirteen is a special year,
so let's have a birthday party for you.'

This is music to my ears.
I've never had a birthday party before.

Mama and I make little sky-blue invites
by hand on colourful construction paper

with indigo and purple sketch pens.
The next day, I go into class to distribute them.

Everyone seems happy to come.
Mohit and Ram and even Shalini

take the invites and smile at me some.
I am so excited, I go after school to buy a cake.

Mama and I decorate the house
with streamers and a big banner

that says 'Happy Thirteenth Birthday'.
We blow up balloons and organise paper plates.

'This,'
I think happily,

as I lay the purple napkins out,
'will be the best birthday ever.'

How was I to know that the Gods
would turn this, too, into a lesson?

If Birthdays Were Movies

Then my thirteenth birthday would be
the one where the outcast girl
has a party and invites everyone in her class,
and they all promise they will come,
but no one shows up.

Daybreak slowly melts into night,
as I sit in front of a sugary cake
in a flavour I don't even like
but everyone else does,
and I refuse to cut it.

Humiliation and hunger
gnaw at my stomach
until I finally give in to my mother's
kindness and we wrap up the food
and return gifts for Damini to take to her village.

The difference between a movie
and real life is: in the movie,
the not-so-popular girl
gets a makeover
and becomes queen bee.

In real life, I just cry myself to sleep.
The movie and real life
do have this in common though:
events like these are the sparks
that turn girls from forgotten festivals
into wildfires and fireworks.

Monday in School

Shalini giggles when I walk in
and whispers dramatically,
'How was your birthday, Paro?'

Before I can say anything at all,
she and Mohit burst out laughing.
My cheeks burn with humiliation.

My hands ball themselves into tight fists
and angry tears threaten to fall,
but I do not allow the dam in me to break.

I will not let them see me cry
because of the pain they have inflicted,
so I fake-smile as widely as I can.

'It was actually amazing,
thank you for asking.'
I take in the satisfaction

of Shalini's annoyed expression
and then I bury my head
in my book,

a present from Mama,
and let it take me far, far away
into a place where closets

lead to lands full of kinder people
and wise queens and lemonade
and Turkish delights and cakes.

Mean

Mama tells me about her schooldays.
She tells me about her friends, and about the mean girls
who turned cruelty to other girls into a fine art.

I ask her curiously, 'Why?'
'That's just how girls are to each other sometimes.'
The way she says it sits heavy on my skin.

You see, some girls in my school like Shalini are changing.
I watch them sharpen their words at both ends,
play target practice with other people's feelings.

Their skirts are hiked up higher than school policy.
They spend time hiding in bathrooms smoking.
'Cool girls' – all nonchalance and eye rolls.

They have become expert marksmen
aiming at the worst of everyone's insecurities.
And still, everyone wants to be around them.

I read somewhere about hostages
who fall in love with their abusers.
It's called a *Patty Hearst* situation.

Or maybe every girl just revolts differently.
Some of us take power back through little revolutions.
Others are taught power is pushing people down,

a different kind of education.
And I would not have minded it
if I wasn't such an easy target.

They baptised me 'Pudge' and 'Fatty'
and 'Whale', words that never harmed me
until they were used like darts aimed straight at my heart.

Weight

If enough magazines say it.
If enough girls in school talk about it.
If enough ads on TV emphasise it.
If enough of my favourite actresses look it.
If enough people tease me 'good-naturedly' about it.
If relatives pinch my plump cheeks hard.
If other people make it my identity.

Tell me how do I stop it

from getting under my skin
from building a house inside my head
from making hunger my best friend
from turning food into the enemy

when it feels like the universe is telling me
the less space I take,
the easier I am to love.

Carbs

'Carbs?' Sunita Auntie says with mischief in her eyes
as she hands over the butter naans to Mama.

We are Sunday afternoons of food and friendship,
old songs on the radio filled with memory.

I watch my mother as she laughs but discreetly
passes the plate along to me without taking any.

Her plate is a small portion of rice and some dal,
but if you look at this table, there is food enough.

Every single auntie is talking about weight loss.
The latest diet fads and how they cut sugar out.

Later, I watch as Mama looks at her appearance
in a stunning black and silver saree and says to herself,

'I've put on so much weight. I should be thinner than this.'
And I cannot imagine how she carried me

AND my little brother in a stomach that flat and small.
How she managed to get into size 6 jeans

just weeks after I was born
and still thinks her body is less

than perfect in every way.
Later, I look at myself in the mirror,

poke at my tummy's baby fat and the cheeks
my aunts used to think were so cute when I was a child

and pinch till they were sore. I sigh and hiss,
'I should be thinner than this.'

And Just Like That

As the night stretched its arms
across a capital that never slept,

the warm desert breeze awoke,
the wind chimes sang again,

and the rain began to dance,
turning the city into an oil painting.

The horizon of roads and traffic glittered
like the jeweled throat

of a queen against the setting glow
of the red, red sun.

The city slowly became a Goddess
in a crimson saree, her eyes full of celestial light,

her stomach round and proud.
Two henna-covered hands held lotuses,

while the other two reached out
and took my own hands as I sat up.

I knew why she was here.
It was time for the fourth story.

The Fourth Story

A long, long time ago, when animals could still talk and this land was pure enough for magic to roam wild, a thousand creatures lived amongst the stars. These celestial beings breathed within a milky ocean that was made by the mother Goddess herself.

When I first opened my eyes, I was a water maiden with stars woven through my waist-length hair, and I swam the sky-waters easily. I nurtured constellations and helped newborn stars breathe their first breaths. No one taught me how to do these things. It was knowledge my spirit was born with. I was alone, but I was never lonely. My work of nurturing such a vast ocean of newborn stars kept me busy.

All this changed one day when the Devi came to visit me. She told me that I had a different destiny. I would be reborn as a Goddess called Lakshmi to bring balance into the universe. She told me, her golden hands on my face, 'You will be loved. You will be revered. But I must take you from everything you consider you love and hold dear.'

She told me that the Devas and the Asuras were going to stir this starry ocean I call my home. That they were going to take everything of value that comes from the churn. 'That includes you, my daughter. But you must not let them lay claim to you. I will send a lotus flower which will take you where you must go.'

As soon as she uttered those words there was a shift. My next memory was full of pain, a pull dragged me from the ocean. I was cold and standing in a world I did not know. Devas and Asuras surrounded me, and I felt their fury, their fight over who got to possess me, the daughter of the sea of milk. As the voices thundered, I felt myself being torn asunder until I saw a bright light that called to me, and I shook myself free to run to the lotus. It was when I sat within its soft pink petals that I finally felt some solace. The flower floated across the sea, lulling me into a gentle sleep.

This is where the stories say Vishnu found me. Each of his footsteps floated over waves as he walked towards me. He offered me his hand and then said, 'Let me give you my protection, Maiden Goddess. Neither Deva nor Asura should have you. The gifts you bring are so powerful that lesser beings do not know how to handle you.'

What the stories do not tell you is how I smiled and stood without his help, my feet supported by the velvet petals of the lotus. How I looked him in the eyes and said, 'I do not need to be saved, my Lord. I will take your hand only as an equal.'

Vishnu's eyes glistened with something unnamed, words appearing at his lips only after some contemplation. 'My destiny is complicated, oh Goddess. If you choose to be with me, you too will have to go through reincarnation after reincarnation.'

I smiled, finally understanding what the Devi meant, and said, 'I did not leave everything I know to go unchallenged.'

And so I came to this, your earth, in many, many incarnations. As Sita, and Rukmini, and Radha – each one changing history slowly in my own way, yet I am only remembered as consort.

There is a hypocrisy here. One that even divine Goddesses must face. People say that when daughters are born, 'Lakshmi ghar aayi hai.' They tell others that prosperity has been brought into their homes, yet so many still privately consider their daughters burdens. They do not even recognise my truest form and my beauty. Here on this land, they paint me thin, skin so pale that it is almost transparent. But tell me, what is the nature of prosperity? What does prosperity look like if not abundant, the way my body has always been. The truest version of me is this: prosperous, full-bodied, skin the colour of the earth in which flowers have just been planted, eyes darker than the storm.

It takes ample arms to hold a newborn star – this they do not consider; weight to tame the wildest of moons when it tries to send the planets out of balance – this they do not consider; hips wide enough to carry a star on while painting a solar system awake. I am larger than life and I love it with the core of my very being.

Which is why I am trying to tell you, dearest girl, if they even try to tame the Goddess of Prosperity into half of her real self by depicting her in a way their small mortal minds find palatable, then they are not worth listening to when nurturing your body, and the way you feel comfortable in your own skin.

Nourish yourself with what you want. I give you permission.

After the Fourth Visit

Paro: Do you ever wish you could live your old life again?

Lakshmi: Goddesses and women live many lives. We cannot go back to who we used to be, only towards who we become.

Paro: But do you?

Lakshmi: Sometimes. We all wish we could walk back sometimes. I am no different.

Paro: Why do the Gods and Goddesses reincarnate?

Lakshmi: So that we fulfil our dharma, our cosmic duty. So that we never forget what it is like to be human. The beauty and tragedy of being mortal is a gift to all, even to the divine.

Paro: How do you cope with the pain of what once was?

Lakshmi: By thinking of the beauty of what will be.

Paro: Do all Gods and Goddesses know the future and what will be?

Lakshmi: Sometimes. Other times, the universe surprises us as much as it surprises you. But we trust and believe that what is coming will bring beauty with it. Like the lotus that grows even in the muddiest of water, every experience brings with it wisdom, virtue and wonder, if you choose to see it.

The Next Day in English Class

Mrs Kamra is small, fierce-eyed,
with henna-red hair in the sunlight.
She looks like a witch escaped from a fairytale.

She reads us Robert Frost and William Wordsworth
and Rabindranath Tagore and says,
'A poem is different for everyone who hears it.'

I raise my hand and ask,
'But, Mrs Kamra, why are all the poets we read men?'
Ram sneers, 'Because women write shit poetry.'

Mohit and the other boys burst into peels of laughter.
Mrs Kamra silences them with THAT glare.
The one where she narrows her eyes till they are small slits,

and if the glare is on you, you feel like a worm.
They shrivel in their seats
and bury their heads in their textbooks.

Mrs Kamra looks at me
and says, 'We read poets selected
in the school syllabus by the board.'

This doesn't answer my question,
but the meaningful look
she gives me, answers everything.

Homework Assignment English Class

For the poetry module we are currently studying, read the work of women who were writing at the same time as the male poets we are studying in the syllabus. Choose a poet you admire and try to write a poem like her. There are many brilliant poets you can read including Sarojini Naidu, Dr Maya Angelou, Audre Lorde, Amrita Pritam, Emily Dickinson, among many others.

Tell Your Daughters

A Poem by Paro Madera After Dr Maya Angelou

Tell your daughters how you love your body.
Tell them how they must love theirs.

Tell them to be proud of every bit of themselves –
from their tiger stripes to the soft flesh of their thighs,
whether there is a little of them or a lot,
whether freckles cover their face or not,
whether their curves are plentiful or slim,
whether their hair is thick, curly, straight, long or short.

Tell them to love the skin they are in,
whether they are fair or dark,
whether they are short, tall, big or thin,
whether they are embarrassed by their scars,
or the blemishes and marks on their skin.

Tell them how beautiful they are
no matter what anyone else says.
Tell them their body isn't flawed
and how it fits them perfectly
in so many thousands of ways.

Tell them how they inherited
their ancestors' souls in their smiles,
that their eyes carry countries
that breathed life into history,
that the swing of their hips
does not determine their destiny.

Tell them never to listen when bodies are critiqued.
Tell them every woman's body is beautiful
because every woman's soul is unique.

Mouth

In the summer of Class Nine,
I am now more mouth than girl.
Everything around me fits badly.
They call me tree
because I'm taller than most of the boys,
and I tell them I love trees.
They call me swordfish
because my nose is so long,
and I tell them so what.
They call me a monster,
and I laugh and say, 'So be afraid.'
I still have thick hair on my legs
while the other girls glimmer
like the stars have sculpted them:
hairless limbs, glowing, petite,
'The way girls should look'.
Even the women's magazines
tell me that I am wrong.
So this is what Papa meant
when he said the world
would make me feel small.

This too is a rite of womanhood.
You are taught in subtle ways to hate yourself
from when you are still a seed.

What choice do I have when I am not hiding,
but to make this tongue so sharp
that everything around me bleeds?

Fourteen

Maybe it is an age thing.
Or maybe it's because of Indra.
Or maybe it was what happened
all those years ago at the bazaar.

But Mama and I just don't talk –
not the way we used to any more.
There are no more bedtime stories
and no lullabies.

Indra was born a worrier
and a chatterbox. He tells Mama
everything, has no secrets,
nothing hidden from her.

She's stricter with me now.
No more dresses or shorts for me.
No more sleeveless T-shirts,
even in the height of summer.

Her eyes are rimmed with sleeplessness.
Raising two children virtually alone
in a city that is not kind to women
is a gamble with the Gods.

Maybe that's why she prays more.
Every morning, she reads
the newspapers, her face paling
at all the rapes in the city.

She reads about weeping mothers.
When I catch her watching me
as I eat my breakfast before school,
I know she is worrying about me.

I Do Indra's Homework for Him

I know I'm not supposed to, but Mama asks me to.
She says I know how to be still and calm
better than he can ever be.

This doesn't strike me as fair
as I have both my and his homework to do
but if it helps her, I say nothing in protest.

I love my brother and he loves me,
but the differences between us
become more obvious every year.

When Indra was a baby, he used to
wrap his fingers around my hair so he could sleep.
Now he talks back to me.

His insults are becoming sharper.
His voice is growing colder.
I try to let it go.

Try to keep doing all the things I used to.
Be the tooth fairy to him,
sometimes get a present because I can.

And even though he still calls me *Didi*
and asks me to read him stories,
I notice he asks for them less,

I notice he gets a far-away look often,
a look of someone older and wiser
lost in his worries.

The Mandir

Every Tuesday morning,
we go to see the Goddess.

'Tuesdays are auspicious,'
Mama says as we cover our heads

and walk the marble stairs barefoot,
the cool welcome in the summer heat.

The pujari is chanting mantras
as we fold our hands, close our eyes and pray.

Well, Mama prays.
I just close my eyes before the statue.

I suppose it's different
when you know She does not look like that,

that the Goddess you know
and the ones others pray to

are completely different
divine beings.

When we leave,
Mama asks me,

'What did you pray for?'
And I swallow hard,

the way I always do before I lie to her.
'I prayed to do well at school.'

An answer that should hopefully satisfy
any mother including my own.

When Papa Is Home from Sailing

He lets Mama sleep in,
and wakes Indra and me
with cups of turmeric milk,
even makes our tiffins.

I may be fourteen,
but he still puts
5 Star chocolates
and Parle-G biscuits in my bag.

He tells us stories of the ship
and all his travels
and makes sure
we have done our homework.

It's how I learn
there are a multitude
of ways
to say I love you.

For so many
you don't
have to use
words at all.

Bullies

Every school has them;
it's not like mine is special.

I don't mind the boys so much any more;
Mohit and Ram are the worst of them.

They pull my ponytail and make fun,
unimaginative jibes that are too dull to be cruel.

It's the girls who really hurt me.
Shalini now has her own clique with Priya and Mahi.

I think they can sense that I am lonely.
In the wrong hands, that is a weapon.

Priya is the leader. Tall with a fringe, razor-smiled
and pretty. Shalini is the cruelest one now,

small with barbed insults, flicking
her long, dark hair at the ready.

Mahi is the oddity. She is kind,
just not when the others are around.

When the three of them are together,
they are the swell of the sea before you drown.

Bucktooth and *Bitch* and *Churel*
fall so easily from their lips.

But when Priya and Shalini are not there,
Mahi sidles up close to me,

shares the strawberries in her lunchbox
with me, but no words.

A secret we do not even speak of to each other.

'What Happened at School Today?' Mama Asks

What I want to say:

I failed in geography even though I studied, I think I may be stupid, and Anu ma'am made me stand outside class for doing my homework wrong and Priya wouldn't stop throwing things at me during assembly's last song and Mohit yanked my hair so hard today a chunk came out in his hand, and my head is still throbbing, and I was mean to a junior student because I was angry and sad, and now I feel terrible about it but I don't know how to say sorry, what should I do? I feel so alone there, don't make me go back, Mama, the children over there, they scare me, they make me want to swallow my own bones, they make me not want to exist any more, my heart is so small and sore.

What I say instead:

Nothing. It was school.

More Things I Do Not Tell Mama

1.

There was a new boy in class today.
His name is Sam, he has dimpled cheeks,
and is Kashmiri like me.

He likes *Star Wars* and speaks with an American accent,
and he draws killer whales and dinosaurs all the time.
They cover every single page of his sketchbook.

He is so talented and strange and clever,
but the other children in class make fun of him.
I think this is how I know we will be friends.

2.

I spend all my breaks in the library
between the pages of old books
that they do not teach us from in class.

I used to prefer reading Jane Austen than studying biology.
But then Miss Walia, the librarian,
introduced me to the feminist mythical retellings
of Dr Chitra Banerjee Divakaruni.

Her version of Draupadi
is truest to the real one
who told me the story
all those years ago.

3.

Every time Shalini and Priya
single me out during break,
I think about the stories
you told me when I was a child.

I think about Nani's cool hand on my forehead.
I wish myself a thousand miles away.
It helps when they turn into hunters.
At least with my knife-mouth I am no longer easy prey.

4.

Mahi sits right next to me in English class,
which is partly why I like it best.

Sometimes when I sneak a look at her,
I meet her eyes because she's already looking at me.

5.

In history class I learn the words
'History is written by the victors'.

When Mrs Krishnan talks about partition,
I feel the rivers of blood in my very bones.

They talk about it so clinically,
like it was so long ago

that a page has been turned,
the chapter a long-forgotten relic.

Sometimes after history class,
I cry in the girls' toilets, whispering,
    my land,
        my family,
            my home.

What They Teach About Partition in School

So it happened like this: the British Raj ended,
but they wouldn't leave the country as it was.

Why? Because of religious tensions
which were leading to bloodshed

and pain and heartache
for Muslims, Hindus, Sikhs.

Why? Because people from different religions
believe in God in different ways.

And sometimes that leads to
misunderstandings and violence.

Did a Muslim, a Hindu and a Sikh draw the line together?
No. It was a British man who had never been east of Paris.

His name was Radcliffe. He was chosen to draw
a line across a map through places he had never visited.

Through Punjab, through Gujarat, through Kashmir,
through Bengal, through Sindh and that became Pakistan.

And a man named Jinnah became their Prime Minister.
And a man named Nehru became ours.

Did this bring peace to all people from both countries?
No. It led to the most violent forced migration in history.

Almost two million people died.
Over seventy thousand women were raped.

Did it at least bring an end to the fighting between us?
No. India and Pakistan are still at odds to this day.

The effects of partition echo for Pakistan, India, Bangladesh.
Millions of families have never recovered.

Was there no way to do this peacefully?
There may have been. But the British were in a hurry.

At the time, they insisted the way they did it
was the best way to do it for us.

The people who colonised our country for over 300 years
claimed they knew what was best for us?

Yes. I know.
It doesn't make any sense to me either.

What I Know About Partition

Sometimes when I look at my grandparents,
I see exactly where Radcliffe drew his line.
Through their lives, through their homes.
Jagged across their hearts.
Crossing over their bones.

I wonder how many families
have been ruined for generations
by a man holding a pen and a map.
I wonder if their faces ever haunted him
as he turned people into numbers and plans.

Partition

A Poem in My History Book by Paro Madera

What my TextBook Says (And I cross out):

~~In 1947, by an act of Parliament of the United Kingdom, British India was divided into two independent countries, India and Pakistan. India is now known as the Republic of India and Pakistan is the Islamic Republic of Pakistan, with Bangladesh becoming the People's Republic of Bangladesh. The idea was to divide two provinces, Bengal and Punjab, based on district-wise non-Muslim or Muslim majorities. This was outlined in the Indian Independence Act 1947, leading to the dissolution of the rule of the British in India, known as the British Raj. India and Pakistan were declared separated on the 15th of August 1947.~~

~~Partition displaced approximately 12 million people, creating a massive refugee crisis in both India and Pakistan, the likes of which had never been seen. Intense violence ensued and close to two million lives were lost. The violence of partition haunts the relationship of India and Pakistan until today, forever creating a rift of distrust between the two countries. The British for their part believe they did right by the two countries because they divided the British Indian Army, the Royal Indian Navy, The Indian Civil Service, the railways and the central treasury between the two.~~

The poem I write over it (and I know to be true):

We called it home till they told us home did not exist any more. Till our neighbours were no longer our friends, till they were the enemies that scorched our houses to the ground, and we had no choice but to run – but where? Did anyone see where the Englishman drew his line? Did they leave anyone here to show us the way out? Is anyone coming to help us? Please. Our people are dying. Their people are dying too. Help us. Help them. We used to be one people, and we are trying not to forget that. Even when the men come with knives and torches, and carry the women away, slaughter the children. This is how the forgetting happens, in the haze of agony. We do to them what they do to us. An eye for an eye: take what they love, burn them the way they burned us until everyone burns. Rage is a wildfire. It races across an imaginary line teaching us all to hate each other. Borders are born from carnage; do not let them lie and tell you the borders were always there. Do not let them trick you into thinking we were just numbers. Not people. We lived too, like you – drenched in memory and family and love and hope and dreams before our lives were dragged from our hands by people we once called friends, people we loved. Is it still called liberty when you rip a country apart so brutally that millions of innocents die? Can a golden bird still fly if you tear her in half? Kashmir. Punjab. Bengal. Gujarat. Sindh. India. Pakistan. Bangladesh. How many brothers and sisters did we lose along the way? This poem could have been written by a Muslim, a Hindu or a Sikh. It does not matter. We all suffered. We all lost people and homes and safety and ourselves along the way. Did anyone ever tell the colonisers that millions of happy families are worth more than billions of ships and trains?

When you look at a map, remember this. Borders are not made of ink, but the wreckage of once-happy families and grief so heavy we have no language to hold it in our mouths. But our people were not made to be held down with the debris you left for us to sift through. Our people were made to rebuild from broken, soar through the skies you took us from.

Nani's Visit

It's not that I'm unhappy to see her,
but seeing Nani in Delhi feels
like watching a kingfisher walk across a road
when it belongs by a river.

It's as though my mind has decided
that if she lives in Paradise House,
that's the only place she exists
in her truest form.

I forget it easily when I feel
the warmth of her hug.
The scent of honey and saffron
clings to her fingers as she cups my face.

And it is then that I realise,
I am so fortunate,
that Heaven itself came
all the way to Delhi to visit.

Nani has travelled
all this way just so
she can celebrate Dussehra
and Diwali with us.

'Has Anyone Ever Told You the Story of Dussehra and Diwali?'

We are sitting at the dining table,
Nani, Mama, Damini and I,
soaking in the September sun
from the big bay window.

Mama is making chocolate ladoos
and rolling them in walnut,
while we are making red and yellow gift boxes
full of almond barfi and sweet samosa.

Damini excitedly claps her hands,
'Ram Sita ki kahani!'
And I grin at her,
'Tell us, please, Nani!'

I have heard the story before
but I love the way Nani tells it.
Mama smiles as she works
and Nani takes a sip of her tea,

and says the most perfect words,
for this Sunday afternoon
full of heartwork.

'Once upon a time ...'

There Lived a Princess

Her name was Sita. It is said that the minute she walked into a room, the calm of a cool breeze followed her footsteps. Legend spread across the land that her mother was actually the Goddess of the Earth, Bhumi, and her royal parents King Janak and his wife Sunaina had found the baby girl in a casket out in the fields.

She grew up with her little sister Urmila, and both girls grew up to care deeply for others. They spent their time using herbs from their own gardens to make poultices and medicines to heal the weak and sick in their kingdom. For a time, all was well.

And perhaps all would have stayed that way if destiny had not intervened. Destiny arrived in the form of a carved ruby-encrusted golden bow that belonged to the Lord Shiva himself. Sita's life was determined in that second. King Janak was to call a swayamvar ceremony for Sita, and all the princes and kings from across the land were invited to win her hand in marriage.

Sita, an obedient daughter, did as she was told.

The challenge was simple. To lift and string Lord Shiva's bow. All who tried it, however, failed. The bow was so heavy no one could lift it, let alone string it. It seemed like no prince or king would ever be able to string the bow. Secretly, Sita was pleased. She wanted to live her contented life with her father, mother and sister, and continue being a healer.

The day was going to draw to a close when a prince walked easily through the crowd of royals. His light shone through the palace, brighter than the sun itself, a serene smile upon his face. Where the other kings were suspicious of each other, in this prince's presence everything seemed to calm.

It took him less than a minute to lift and string the bow. And then, he kept pulling until, with an almighty thunderous crack, the bow broke and fell to pieces.

Sita stepped forwards. There is an old saying, that when you meet your soulmate, your heart will not palpitate. Your body will not grow hot. Instead, you will feel like suddenly, you understand everything, and the tranquillity of a thousand moons will grow between you. That was how she felt when she saw him.

He reached out to her, and this is how Prince Rama, heir to the kingdom of Ayodhya, took Sita's hand.

Misfortune often follows those who choose the nobler, more honourable path in life. Such is the story of Prince Rama. His father, King Dasharatha, had three wives. Kaushalya, Rama's mother, Kaikeyi, mother of Bharata and finally Sumitra, mother to twins Lakshmana and Shatrughna's mother. In Ayodhya, too, the four young princes, who loved each dearly, had brought great peace.

Unfortunately, it was not meant to be. Kaikeyi, the king's favourite queen was unhappy about the fact that Rama would be king and not her son Bharata. So she invoked an old boon she had kept from when she had rescued the king from battle years ago. The day before Rama's coronation, she demanded that, in order to honour the promise he made to her, King Dasharatha would give the throne to her son, and send Rama away, into exile in the forest for fourteen years.

'But Nani, Why Was Kaikeyi Like That?'

I had a habit of interrupting
stories with questions,
and Mama shook her head, frowning at me.

Nani came out of her reverie,
and took another careful sip of her tea.
'I think it was because

she was afraid to lose influence.
People become very dangerous
when they lose power.

Especially when they lack empathy and foresight.'
I nodded solemnly at this.
'Tell us, Nani, what happened next?'

She smiled, and I noticed that despite
the cup having sat beside her for an hour,
the steam still rose like the tendrils of this story.

What Happened Next: The Ramayana

Rama accepted his fate with such grace, Kaikeyi was almost embarrassed. But not enough to take her wish back.

Sita, a good wife, gave up everything too, so she could follow her husband into the forest.

Lakshmana would not let them go alone so he left with them too. The truth is, the Ramayana would not be the epic story it is with Sita and Lakshmana. Their bond was made from friendship, love and family.

But their royalty seemed like a distant dream in the forest of mysteries. Along with the deer and tigers, there also hid Asuras and other forest spirits. Still, the three built a home for themselves, found and ate what they could, met with sages and drew from their wisdom.

The truth is, any hardship is bearable if you have someone to share it with, and that is what Rama, Sita and Lakshmana did.

The years passed. Until one day, while she was washing her laundry in the river, Sita saw the most magnificent golden deer rush past her. Something strange came over her. It was as though all her hopes were pinned on having that deer. It was so unlike her; she was such a selfless person that she was uncomfortable.

But no matter what she did, she could not stop thinking of the deer. So when she returned to the cottage, she told Rama she had to have it. And because Rama loved Sita deeply and knew it was not in her nature to ask for anything, he agreed to get it for her. Hours passed, and Lakshmana and Sita started to grow worried. Almost as if the forest of secrets had heard them, they heard Rama's voice cry out for help. Lakshmana was reluctant to go but Sita made him go. 'My husband, your brother needs you!'

He drew what is called the Lakshmana Rekha around the house, and told her, 'Sister, do not step out of this line, please.'

Sita agreed, and Lakshmana left to find his brother. It was not an hour after he had left when a sage came to the door. You know as well as I do that guests must be taken care of, as if the Gods and Goddesses themselves have walked to your door. So Sita did her duty. She brought food to the sage, but due to the line, the sage could not cross it. He told Sita, 'If you do not feed me, great misfortune will befall your family.'

Sita was an obedient daughter and a good wife, so she did what she was told.

The sage turned into Ravana, the King of Lanka, with demonic strength, and he kidnapped Sita and took her away on his flying chariot. Sita cried out for help, fought Ravana the entire way, but it was useless. Once there, Ravana told Sita he wanted her to be his wife. She refused and resisted him, so he imprisoned her in a palace garden with the highest of walls. Every day, he visited her to demand that she marry him and she refused him. Every day, Sita told him she would never. No amount of threats would change her mind. One day, when Sita was sitting under the shade of a tree, dreaming of her life before, Hanuman the flying monkey God landed before her. He told her that Rama was on his way to rescue her, but he could carry her to him.

Sita was a good wife. She knew that her rescue meant honour being restored to Rama. So she refused Hanuman and he flew back to Rama and delivered her message.

Not long after that, the war between Rama and Ravana began. As wars often are, there was immense and needless loss of life on both sides. Family members died. Ravana lost his son. Finally unable to bear so much loss of life, Rama fought Ravana on the battlefield alone, where Ravana assumed his full ten-headed demonic form. Eventually Rama killed Ravana, and this is the victory we celebrate as Dussehra, when we burn effigies of Ravana, to symbolise burning evil away. Sita is finally reunited with Rama, but sadly there is no joy to this reunion yet. Rama asked her for an Agni Pariksha, a test of fire, to prove her chastity for the year she had lived in the home of another man. The horror at having to prove herself to her husband, when she had been imprisoned against her will, devastated Sita. Even Lakshmana was shocked at his brother's request.

But Sita was a good wife, and did as she was told. A fire was lit and she walked into the flames. Agni, the God of Fire, brought her out whole as she was chaste. And Rama embraced her, and finally, all of them made the long trip back to Ayodhya as Rama's exile was complete. This is why, twenty-one days later, we celebrate the festival of lights, Diwali, for when Prince Rama, who will be King Rama, returns, and Ayodhya, in joy, lit up every candle, every diya to symbolise the return of Prince Rama, the light to their kingdom.

There is another version of the tale, where finally Sita chose herself, and after walking through the flames returned to Bhumi, her mother, instead of her husband. But that is the tale they do not like to tell. After all, it doesn't make for a happy ending to them when a woman is able to stand up to years of patriarchal oppression with a simple phrase: 'No more.'

Later On, After the Story, Nani Asks

Do you have many friends here?

I swallow hard,
shake my head.

Why is that?

I don't know anyone kind.
Everyone in my school is mean.

All of them?

Yes,
all of them.

Do you know why you want a friend?

Why I want a friend?
What does that mean?

Lo, dekho.
How are you going
to find a friend
if you do not know
what you are looking for?

Friendship: A Checklist

I want a friendship
as lively as my mother's best friend's
eyes in her wedding photos.

A friendship
so astronomical
that it puts galaxies to shame.

A friendship
with a texture so rare that Halley's Comet
feels like an everyday occurrence.

A friendship
before which the sun
himself pales.

A friendship
soft enough to weep into,
the way newborn stars wept in Lakshmi's arms.

But also a friendship
tough enough to weather
all of this school's quiet harms.

Is this too much to ask for?
Perhaps, perhaps it is.
If none of these work,

then I hope for a friendship
where we can make each other laugh
and love all the colours we see in each other,

on the days
we are rainbows
as much as on the days we are shades of grey.

The Introvert Tries to Make a Friend

I could say,
'Hi, what are you drawing?'
(too nosy)

Or I could say,
'Hello, my name is Paro.'
(too formal)

Or I could say,
'Did you do the maths homework?'
(too nerdy)

Or I could say,
'How are—'

'Hi.' A voice makes me jump so high
I drop the water I am swigging
all over my maths textbook and squeal.

The person next to me bellows with laughter,
and it's so infectious I can't help but join in.
'Sorry. I'm Sam.' He smiles a dimpled smile. 'Paro, right?'

I nod, still shaking out my textbook.
He takes it from my hands.
'Here.' He takes out a handkerchief. 'Let me help.'

Sam Writes Notes to Me

Sam: Did you know that otters
hold hands when they sleep
so they don't drift away?

Paro: No, I didn't.
Do you believe that animals
feel as much love as humans do?

Sam: Yes. Did you know that birds
are the closest living relatives
to the dinosaurs?

Paro: Does this mean
I can call chickens
Cluckosaurus Rexes?

Sam: You're so funny.
That should totally be
their official name.

Paro: Do you want
to go to the library after—

The paper is snatched
from my hand
by Mrs Krishnan.

'Paro,
who are you
writing to?'

I sit there, my heart thudding.
Thirty-one pairs of eyes on me,
and I look down, lips sealed.

'Tell me right now.'
I quietly look down at my hands
as pin-drop silence swells in the classroom.

'If you're not going to tell me,
you can stand outside class
for the rest of the lesson.'

She balls up the paper
and throws it in my direction.
'Dafa ho jao. OUT.'

And as I get up,
staring at my feet,
a table shifts behind me.

'Ma'am, it was me,'
a voice says softly;
and I turn to see Sam standing.

'Then YOU can get out too!'
shouts Mrs Krishnan,
pointing us both to the door.

Once we are outside though,
and the door is safely shut,
our eyes meet and we dissolve into giggles.

My Nani Is Magic

And I know this because
when I run home
from the bus stop that day
to tell her all about Sam,
she is already waiting for me
at the door, chocolate cake in hand.
She listens with a knowing smile
as I tell her all about my day,
and later, I hear her as she prays,
'Thank you, Devi Ma,
for the happiness you brought
my granddaughter's way.'

Visiting Sam's House

When Sam invites me over,
I nervously ask Mama if she could take me.
She says yes and gets the car keys quickly.

'I'm so happy you've made a friend.'
'It's not a big deal,' I tell her,
but the truth is, it means a lot to me.

Sam's house wasn't far from ours,
and Mama was going to come in to meet his mother,
especially after I told her they were Kashmiri.

We stop at a blue bungalow with climbing pink
bougainvillea and a lady in a pink saree that matches
the bougainvillea answers the door and greets us warmly.

'Hello, beautiful girl, you must be Paro.'
I smile so hard my face hurts.
'Hello, auntie! This is my Mama!'

Auntie asks Mama to stay for chai,
We sit in an elegant drawing room with walls painted cream,
filled with huge oil paintings of rural village scenes.

Every porcelain table top is covered with photos of family.
The sofas have been carefully selected
to be the exact same shade of white as the carpet.

Sam's house reminds me of Shalini's, but much more welcoming.
Sam materialises on the wooden staircase in jeans
and a Teenage Mutant Ninja Turtles T-shirt.

We both realise at the same time that
we are wearing exactly the same outfit,
and all of us burst out laughing.

Mama notices Sam's sketchbook first.
'May I see it?' A look from his mother
prompts him to show it to her.

'Wow,' Mama says as she looks through
the skilful sketches of dinosaurs and whales.
'Are you going to university to be an artist?'

An unease flickers across Sam's face,
but before he can answer, his mother says,
'Actually, Samarth is going to be a doctor.'

Mama looks impressed. I am more worried
about my friend because his smile now seems forced.
'Sam, can you show me more of your work?' I ask.

He looks relieved. 'Sure! Follow me!'
His mother calls after us, 'Leave the room door open –
you know the rules, Samraj! And get Paro a soft drink!'

We bound up the stairs and through the first door on top.
When he opens the door, I gasp.
The walls are covered in sketch after sketch,

and even though the bed isn't made,
and there are clothes on the floor,
all I can see is the terrifying T. rexes,

and the gentle blue whales,
and the dancing orcas and their babies.
'Hey Paro!' Sam says, and I turn.

He tosses me a sketchbook
and a pencil that I just barely catch,
'Want to draw?' he asks.

And that is how I met a great love of my life:
drawing, sketching, art.

Fifteen

This is the last year you will play Holi.

Don't panic. Breathe. This will be the most important lesson you will learn this year. You know why you go to play Holi. This is a joy of a festival the welcoming of spring where everyone dances and plays with a thousand different colours, pitchkaris, water balloons and laughter. You love the colours, you love meeting your extended family. And you love the story behind it. The one where a tyrannical king declares himself a God because he thinks he has obtained immortality, and his son refuses to worship him and only worships the Gods he believes in – and though his father sends his aunt to kill him, the boy's unwavering belief in both God and himself protects him. The problem is, you do not like being touched, still. And Holi cannot be celebrated without skin meeting skin. How else does one smear colour on another's face. You've always been afraid to say no. But that morning when your parents are waiting for you, you tell them, *I don't want to go.* And they insist. And your brother insists. But you say no, until they finally hear it. When they leave, you will go to your room and pull out the sketchbook your brother gave you, and start drawing. In that moment you will realise that sometimes the choices you make to be comfortable will feel distant from the choices of the people you love. That you are changing. And this is fine, because evolution is both quiet and fraught – often practised in silence, the same silence in which the stars are born. You will be forced to face more this year that you wished to keep secret. You will know love in the most painful of ways. You are oversensitive and others will hurt you, because you still haven't learned to harden your heart. As you draw, you will think about the way your parents love each other. How often they fight and what they fight about (mostly it's you and your brother). The way your father cares for your mother when she is sick. The way he treats her parents like they are his own. The way she does the same. You will wonder if you could ever have a love like that. This is what you don't know yet: girlhood is an act of survival this year. Girlhood is confronting the parts of you that you think are too dark for anyone to love.

This will be the last time you celebrate Holi. But this is also the first year you have stood up for yourself. And even though you did, and even though you let your parents down, the world did not fall apart like you always thought it would.

Sports Day

It is sports day, and I am not sporty.
I am all gangly and overgrown
like the wild grass just beyond the field,
but the PE teacher refuses to give up on me.
Sonam ma'am is persistent,
the daughter of a general;
giving up isn't part of her language.
She truly believes she can mould
a sportswoman out of me yet.

'Paro, you have the height for it!'
she says as she pushes me towards
all these daunting things.
I fail miserably at basketball.
Have you ever seen a five-foot-eight thing fall?
It turns out it's really quite funny.
I absolutely lack the coordination for football.
Even as goalie, all I do is get the wind
knocked out of me.

But a good teacher doesn't give up,
not when she sees potential in a kid.
So she makes me race and cycle
and swim until she realises
I am terrible at all of it.
Finally, she makes me stand in line
somewhere, saying,
'Long jump. Try this, and if you cannot,
I promise I will let you go.'

What she means is,
she will give up.
And maybe it is the way
her fingers grip her clipboard
when she says it, or the fact
that I cannot take another adult

abandoning me,
but I close my eyes and run,

     leap through

              what feels like

                         skies

… and come away with a bronze medal,
but more importantly to me at the time,

the approval in her eyes.

The Girls' Cloakroom

I don't see Mahi at break any more.
We don't share tiffins
or speak or even make eye contact.

So when she corners me on sports day
in the cloakroom, I am halfway certain
she's going to hurt me somehow.

She hangs out with the mean girls after all,
but she simply pushes me into the cloakroom
and closes the door.

'Why won't you eat lunch with me any more?'
 she asks, arms crossed,
and I lose my voice for a minute.

Finally I look her in the eyes, frown and say,
'I don't need your pity.
I have a real friend now.'

She looks surprised,
her fringe a mess of sweat
from all the sprinting she has done today.

'I don't pity you.
Where did you get
that idea from?'

It's the way she looks at me.
All heart-shape-faced
and big doe eyes.

My palms sweat.
My heart beats so fast.
She makes me feel like I am drowning inside.

I only avoid her truly
because
I need to survive.

'Paro,' she steps closer to me;
I can smell her scent so strongly.
She always smells of strawberries

even in the wintriest of winters.
She smells like summer and rain.
'Tell me,' she asks again, too close, too close.

My lungs feel like they are filling with water.
'Why do you think I pity you?'
I feel a bit dizzy.

We are so close I can feel the heat from her skin
– and then she reaches out.
Her hand touches my arm and

I yelp like lightning
has passed through me.
Push her away.

And run.

The Thing Is

There is a secret sapling in me that I refuse to water.
I felt it growing in me when I was ten years old
and an actress danced with a hero I cannot remember.
She made my head spin like a merry-go-round.
The way she moved her hips had me spellbound.
I thought about what I saw at my cousin's wedding.
I thought about how no one speaks of her any more.
Every time I do, the fear teaches me
how to push my feelings further down.
Still. Curiosity makes me want to know.
When I looked up 'girls that like girls'
on the family computer
in the living room, I found nothing
but naked women in the throes of passion.
My face turned so very red,
I closed the window down at lightning speed.
I spent the next week jumping every time
someone mentioned my name.
'Paro!' – even my own name sounded like sin.
'Paro!' – I looked for disappointment within my own name.
'Paro!' – I felt like a question mark each time someone called me
by my own name.

I feel the roots digging firmer into me today.
She said my name that way.
All tender like a newborn rose.
What if someone saw us?
Would they smell the stink of want on me?
What would they say if they did?
What would *everyone* think?

There is a secret sapling in me I refuse to water.
And still … it persists.

The Text

For my fifteenth birthday,
my parents bought me a cell phone.
Mama said, 'In case you get lost or hurt,
it would be useful to have with you.'

I think of it more like a tracking device.
So I avoid it on most days.
Only four numbers exist on there anyway.
Mama, Papa, Nani, Sam.

I have never needed it really until today.
Today as I sit at home and watch a movie
with Damini and we both giggle like
we are conspiring at Govinda's comedy.

The phone beeps. And I pick it up,
expecting my mother.
Instead, I see a text
from an unknown number.

'Hi Paro, I got your number from Sam.
I just wanted to say I am sorry if I ever
did something to hurt you. I would like us
to be friends. Can we be friends? Mahi.'

I swallow hard and mentally
make a note to kill Sam.
A thousand things
run through my head.

Instead I message her back
In the evening:
'Hi Mahi. Of course we can be friends.
Paro.'

'What Are You Smiling At?' Mama Asks
Gently As She Dresses Indra for School

Indra is in a silly mood.
His mischief is how
he earned his nickname
'Hanuman' after the Monkey God.

He is absolutely not cooperating.
I laugh as he runs around my legs,
still in his vest. He is nine,
but he acts younger,

partly because I encourage him
to be that way,
partly because Mama
doesn't want him growing up either.

I put away the phone
into my skirt pocket
and smile at her.
'Nothing.'

Mama looks at me
with a raised eyebrow,
and for a moment
I think she may ask for my phone.

But right then,
there is a loud bang in the kitchen
and Damini shouts 'BABA!'
as Indra cackles

and like a whirlwind, my mother is gone.

We Text Every Day Now

Mahi: hi. you still up?

Paro: yep, was just gonna go to bed

Mahi: you coming to school tomorrow?

Paro: :/ when do I ever miss school?

Mahi: it's true, you're a huge nerd

Paro: i am not! you're the one who is always like, mrs krishnan, you're so clever, oh mrs agnihotri, let me get you some tea!

Mahi: >.< i do not talk like that, you make me sound like a big kiss ass

Paro: you are though

Mahi: i'm not

Paro: uh oh, two word texts, are you grumpy with me?

Mahi: maybe

Paro: you're not a kiss ass. but you ARE cute when you pout

Mahi: not fair! lol! i'm mad at you, stop flirting with me. :P

Paro: ;)

Mahi: can i ask you something?

Paro: yes. always

Mahi: you promise you won't mind?

Paro: you're making me nervous now, lol

Mahi: why do you always look so uncomfortable in biology class?

Paro: … it's a long story

Mahi: want to tell me about it in dilli haat tomorrow?

Paro: what … mahi, are you saying we bunk class?

Mahi: come on, have you never done that before? come on. lets skip bio and go to dilli haat. i promise it will be fun.

Paro: lol okay. lets do it. you will have to show me though.

Mahi: show you what.

Paro: how to bunk class.

Mahi: lmao, see? huge nerd.

Paro: shut up lol. see you tomorrow!

Mahi: goodnight :*

Paro: goodnight :* :*

DELETE ALL MESSAGES?

DELETED

The Trouble Is, Biology Class Reminds Me Too Closely of Shame

It tells me there is too much flesh everywhere.
Dust particles are dead skin, fruit is flesh too.

And the apple I eat after school that day
says I am no better than fruit.

I am apple, cherry, peach
and apricots too.

But that means I am apple seeds,
cherry, peach and apricot pits.

You know what they say
in some religions

about apples and women.
We have complicated relationships.

I'm still trying so hard to make sense of what he did.
The Man with the Brutal Hands.

He saw my flesh
and thought of me like the fruit he sold.

Something to be taken.
Something to be bitten into.

Biology class says he was right,
but it also says

apples hide cyanide in their seeds,
behind the most innocent of guises.

Maybe if you grind up my bones,
you would find poison in there too.

In the Autorickshaw

I am still breathless.
Mahi's musical laugh mixes
with the pandemonium of Delhi traffic.

We sneaked out through sick notes
that Mahi forged, and once out of the school gate
Mahi is the one who caught us the rickshaw.

'I can't believe you've never done this before!'
she giggles at my panicked face but her fingers
ease around my clenched hand to reassure me.

'Mahi, what if we get caught?!'
I shout over the roar of the rickshaw
'We won't,' she says easily.

'Look! It's India Gate!'
I follow her line of sight to the pale red granite
memorial to soldiers of World War I,

covered in the names of people
who were loved, and I wonder
how often people are spoken of after they die.

I am about to say this to Mahi
when I notice that the rickshaw driver,
a kind-eyed man with an infectious laugh

has only two photos in his rickshaw.
One of a small, sweet girl in plaits in a school uniform.
And right next to her the Goddess Lakshmi.

I think it's sweet how sometimes
When he stops at a traffic light,
He looks at his daughter's photo with such love.

I imagine that when the days are particularly hard,
he looks at that photo and thinks
'This is for you. All of this is for you.'

And she gives him the strength
to get through
each one of his days.

'You're so quiet,' Mahi observes.
'I'm just thinking,' I answer.
'About your next poem?' Her tone is teasing.

I go bright red, my heart rate rising.
'How did you know?'
I thought I hid my poems well.

Her eyes dance as she presses her finger to her lips.
'It's a secret.' I bump her shoulder with mine,
and we both laugh.

Finally she says, 'If you let me, I'd love to read your poetry.'

Dilli Haat

Is the only bazaar I have ever gone to
since I was seven, and maybe that's because
it's a bazaar full of artists and crafts people.

Phirans from Kashmir, Madhubani paintings,
shawls from Nagaland and beautiful wood carvings
make this a safer place for me, but still,

I hold on to Mahi's hand as we weave
around people in the crowd, pausing
first at a handmade jewellery store.

Everything here is sterling silver,
and Mahi tries on a thumb ring where
the silver leaves twist delicately around her thumb.

It looks beautiful against her dark skin,
but when we hear the price, she baulks
and puts it back and we go wander around some more.

I wait until she has disappeared to the toilet,
and with my heart thudding in my ears,
I decide to face my fear and be brave.

I walk back alone to the store
and use all the pocket money I've saved from
the last six months to buy her the ring.

When Mahi finds me, I am shaking,
more from being alone in the crowd
than my impulse purchase.

But when I press it into her hand gently,
her sparkling eyes and joyful squeal
makes it all worth it.

Momos and Shalini

We are sharing vegetarian momos in the food market,
sitting on a rickety wooden table when I finally ask her,
'Mahi, why do you hang out with Shalini and Priya?
They're both so mean and you just aren't.'

Mahi tilts her head and looks at me,
licking chilli sauce from her thumb
with the ring on, 'Priya is odd,
but, Paro, I don't think you understand Shalini.'

I rolled my eyes. 'She's bullied me for years, Mahi.
What is her problem? Her mother is great,
she never wants for anything, and she always
gets best marks in every class in school.'

Mahi raises an eyebrow. 'Paro,
why do you think she does so well in school?'
I shrug. 'She wants to get into a good university?'
Mahi shakes her head and says,

'Here is the thing you don't know about Shalini.
She's a really lonely person. Her mother is never home,
her father works all the time, and she has no grandparents.
She aces every class in school just so her parents notice her.

And they never *ever* do.'

This unsettles me deeply.
Sunita Auntie seems so nice,
but now that I think about it I realise I haven't
ever seen her hug or even smile at Shalini,

not once in the hundreds of Sundays
we have spent at each other's homes.

The Sketch

Mahi is still hungry, so she buys
spicy potatoes with more chilli sauce,
and as she eats and talks, and I listen,
I pull out my sketchbook to draw her, just like that.

Her skin glowing in the gaze of the sun
highlighting her perfect cheekbones,
her wild hair coming loose from her ponytail,
a laugh caught in her eyes and—

'What are you drawing?'

'Nothing!' I close the sketchbook
and put my elbow on it.
'Show me!' She giggles and yanks it out
from under my arm.

I watch the joy die in her eyes,
but her lips say, 'This is pretty, Paro.'
I notice the sadness in her downturned mouth.
'Did I do something wrong?'

'No, it's not you – this is nice.
It just reminds me of something.'
Worry clamps around my heart.
'Tell me what it is, and I'll fix it.'

Mahi stares at me. 'That's just it, Paro – *you* can't.'
I am confused and it must show on my face because she says,
'Has your mother ever left fairness creams
on your dressing table? Have old aunties

every loudly commented on your dark complexion
and said how hard it will be to find you a husband?
Have you never seen the fairness cream ads
that show how when the dark-skinned girl

becomes fair, people finally think she is beautiful?

Have your favourite actresses
and actors all participated in an ad
that makes you feel like you aren't beautiful
because of how dark you are?'

I am appalled. She's right.
I've never known any of this
and say the first thing I can think of,
'Mahi. You're beautiful despite any of that.'

She stares at me and says
with truth and pride in every word.
'Fuck your "despite", Paro.
I want to be loved *because* of my skin.

The Goddesses have skin like mine.
I am earth and night sky.
Why shouldn't this skin be known as beautiful too?
It is to me. It should be to you.'

I look down at the sketch
and back at her,
'But, Mahi, you *are* beautiful as you are.
You always will be to me.'

She points to the sketch
as she looks directly into my eyes.
'If you believe that, Paro,
then why did you draw me so light-skinned.'

Coming Home

We don't speak much on the auto ride back.
Mahi is contemplative, and even though I fixed the sketch,
she doesn't feel like talking and I can respect that.

When we reach school, we take different autos home.
And I make sure I only start walking home
from the bus stop when the school bus leaves.

I'm trying to think about how to make it up
to Mahi when Mama opens the door in a panic.
'I'm so glad you're home, Paro.

Go sit with Damini.'
And she grabs her car keys and is gone.
I hear a soft sob in the kitchen,

and go to see Damini sitting on the floor,
her arms around her knees, crying inconsolably.
'Didi! Kya hua?!' I am on the floor beside her,

and I wrap my arms around her as she weeps.
Damini tells me her father was beating her mother,
and when she tried to intervene, he hit her so hard

she fell against the wall and hurt her head.
I noticed the bandage when she says this
and instantly got up and got her a glass of water.

We sit there, and she cries, 'What if he kills her?'
I say comfortingly, 'Mama won't let that happen.'
And I pray that I am right.

We sit like that for what feels like hours,
and then Mama walks into the kitchen.
Behind her is a small woman in a yellow saree.

Her lip is swollen and her arm is in a cast.
But she is does not look sad, instead she smiles
when she sees her daughter.

'Ma!' Damini runs over and hugs her so hard
I hear her mother squeak.
Mama says to me softly,

'From now on, Damini and her mother
will be living with us,
Damini's mother and I

are going to set up an embroidery business
together till she can run it alone.
And Damini will go to school.'

I learn that day
just how someone can use their privilege
to champion others and help them rise too.

Later in My Room, I Write a Poem for Mahi

Did you know that Sappho
wrote all her poems to girls too?
She wrote them sweet-apple perfect,
wild hyacinth flower, purple-blossomed,
and I know she was talking about you.

You, a wild-eyed Devi,
sitting among us mortals,
thinking no one has noticed your beauty yet.
But it is hard to hide splendour like yours
when it is a gift from divinity.

Let me worship at your altar.
Let me show you what I see,
gentle Goddess.
You do not need to become one of us.
Let me show you what you were born to be.

I don't know
how to love people well yet.
But I know I can love you
the way you deserve
if you let me.

Search History

Search: can a girl love another girl
Search: is there a name for girls loving girls
Search: how to know if you are a lesbian
Search: what if you like boys and girls
Search: what group do you belong to if you like boys and girls
Search: bisexual girls
Search: bisexual girls not porn
Search: how to block porn when you search for something
Search: what does two or more genders mean
Search: how many genders are there
Search: lesbian and gay information
Search: LGBT community Delhi
Search: LGBT community India
Search: what is section 377 of the Indian Penal code
Search: could I get arrested for being bisexual
Search: why are people mean to LGBT people
Search: AIDS crisis in LGBT community
Search: how many LGBT people have died of AIDS so far
Search: will my parents still love me if I'm bisexual
Search: is it safer to keep my sexuality secret if I'm LGBT
Search: hate crimes against the LGBT
Search: hate crimes against bisexual people
Search: why are bisexual women more likely to be raped
Search: are we born gay
Search: if I love a man will this make me straight
Search: how to accept yourself if you are bisexual
Search: is being bisexual bad
Search: can sexual assault make you bisexual/gay/lesbian
Search: are you still allowed to love yourself if you are gay
Search: what are my options if my family disowns me
Search: how to come out without hurting people I love
Search: are all the gods and goddesses straight?
Search: LGBT Hindu goddesses and gods

I Waited

You see, I had become used to it.

When I felt that pain in my chest,
when I felt like I was made of worry and fret,
when I felt like I was drowning,

they always came to visit.

So I waited for the sun to set,
and for the night to transform the city
into a festival of lights and shadows.

I waited,
and waited,
and waited

until the sun
kissed the sky awake.
But the Goddess never came.

The Next Day

I am in English class watching the ocean come towards me in the shape of a girl with skin that glows like onyx, eyes like sparkling pearls. No one teaches me that this too is what sinking feels like. That the water would rise over my head and I would let it because it was her. I can't hear the teacher over the din of the waves inside my own head, as she sits beside me, gently places her hand right next to mine so they are touching in a way no one else can see. But these feelings are too big for a fifteen-year-old body. These feelings are Not Indian. I know that now. These feelings are Not Normal, the internet said. But, my God, the more I feel her skin against mine, the more I think: *'No one told me love could be a God of both living and dying. That girls who love girls do not just drown, they also float.'*

Passing Notes Again

Sam: Where have you been? I haven't seen you in days.

I think: *I've been avoiding you so you don't have to see the mess I have become. I think I may be bisexual. I don't know how to tell you. I am afraid of losing you. My choice is either I am a bad friend to you or I risk you being a bad friend to me. So I chose to do this instead, selfishly.*

I write: Studying for the exams. Sorry.

The Art Classroom

In English class,
I finally did it.
I pass Mahi a note that reads:

'Meet me at the grey staircase during PE.'

I want to give her the poem,
somewhere quiet where no one can see us,
because poems, I decide, are a private thing.

My heart thuds as I watch her open it,
and I let out a huge sigh of relief
when I see her smile slightly at me and nod.

So we skip PE.
I tell Sonam ma'am
I have a headache.

Mahi tells her
that her asthma
is acting up.

We are careful.
We climb the grey-tiled staircase
all the way to the art classroom.

It is serenely quiet.
Not a single one of
the ugly florescent lights on.

I am nervous
and looking away from her,
and just as I think of something to say,

she takes my clammy hand,
turns me around so fast
I can barely breathe,

and then her lips are on mine.
Her lips are on mine,
and my whole body freezes.

I didn't even know how much
I wanted to kiss her
until she kissed me first.

And it feels like every star
in the night sky is between
her soft, warm lips pressed against mine.

My arms lock around her waist
and I pull her close,
and she smiles against my mouth.

Her hands rise till I feel her fingers
running through my hair,
sending shudders down my spine,

and when her free hand touches my face
my body feels like I am a boat
and she is the ocean I belong to.

And then suddenly: *BAM!*
The door slams open
and we break apart in terror,

but it is far too late.

That Face

The face you make
when you drink bitter gourd juice
and nearly gag and spit it out.

The face you make
when you smell
rotting vegetables in the bin.

The face your mother makes
when she sees something dreadful
on the news.

The face your father
has when he reads
about politics.

It's sudden and visceral.
It's violent and disgusted.
It's the face Sonam ma'am has

when she looks at us.

The Walk After

'Principal's office. Now.'

Mahi and I don't look at each other.
How do you look at someone
when you feel like a wound made of shame?

It feels like we are strangers
at the mercy of a stranger.
A stranger that was once our favourite teacher.

What Happens Next

In a fairytale
the hero always wins.
In a fairytale
the prince saves the princess.
In a fairytale
you have once upon a times
and happily ever afters.
The prince and princess
end up together.
The villains face their karma.
Almost everyone walks away
with a smile on their face.

But this is no fairytale.
There is no prince in this tale.
We thought we could do without one.
It turns out the world
doesn't feel the same way.
Because our world
doesn't have dragons
or monsters to kill,
but people. Just people.
People who should care
like teachers and parents.
People who should show mercy.
Yet don't.

But as Mahi and I sit outside
the Principal's office waiting
for Sonam ma'am to come out,
I sneak a look at her.
Tears streaming down her face.
White knuckles clenching the bench.

My heart aches and
I reach out to soothe her,
but she violently slaps
my hand away. I pull it back
as white hot shock travels
up my arm, paling my face.
Her dark eyes a tornado,
she glares at me.
Her once soft mouth
is now a wolf snarl.
She barks loudly,
'Get away from me!
Don't you think
you've done enough?!'

If the Universe Was Fair

We wouldn't have been caught.
We would have left the art room giggling,
hand in hand until we came to the staircase,
maybe kissed again before we parted ways.
No. If the universe was fair,
we would have kissed
and not parted ways at all.
We would have met in
the girls' bathroom after class,
and texted each other the rest of the day.
We wouldn't be sitting here
in a cold, lonely corridor,
on this creaky old bench.
We would be in class,
smiling about our hidden secret.
And Mahi would have looked at me
like she could fall in love with me still.
And not like I was the worst thing
that had ever happened to her.

Inside the Lion's Den

What Mr Sharma calls it:
'Inappropriate behaviour.'

What he means:
'Indecent and unforgivable.'

What Mr Sharma says to me:
'I expect better from you.'

What he means:
'This is unacceptable from anyone.'

What Mr Sharma says to Mama:
'Girls from decent houses do not do this.'

What he means:
'There must be something wrong with
the way you brought her up.'

What Mr Sharma says to Papa:
'Being around women all the time can do this.'

What he means:
'Somehow this is your wife's fault.'

What Mr Sharma says to me:
'You should know the police can get involved.'

What he means:
'I could have you arrested under Section 377.'

What Mr Sharma says in the end:
'Paro is a good student.

We are willing to try again
but this is her last chance.'

What he leaves unsaid:
'If she does anything like this again,

she will find there is no mercy
for people like her here.'

On the Car Ride Home

They don't speak to me.
Not Mama, not Papa.
They stare ahead at the road
like statues in the park.

Indra is oblivious.
He chatters on
about his day,
and I answer him,

but my mother's shoulders
stiffen every time I speak.
I can see them so clearly
from where I sit in the backseat.

Like she has something to say.
But she has lost the words.
Is this what it feels like to be suspended
in ice water and left there indefinitely?

The cars inch by us so slowly.
The road home is years long.

In My Room

I keep waiting for my parents
to come and talk to me,
to ask me why I did it,
to tell me I have shamed them,

but as day turns to night
outside my bedroom window,
no one comes to knock.
No one says a thing.

To Mahi

An Apology Poem from Paro

If an apology was easy,
maybe people would do it more often.
I don't know why I'm apologising;
maybe that's a problem.
I just don't like seeing you hurt.

I shouldn't have asked you
to the art classroom.
I thought it was safe.
This was the biggest mistake I made.
Please don't hate me.

You mean the world to me.
I just want you to know that.
You don't have to care for me,
or accept my apology,
but just know, I love you.

Dreams

Hunger spun nightmares.
Every one of them about
Mahi slapping me with her hateful gaze.
Mama telling me she hates me.
Papa telling me he cannot love me.
Indra disappears and I never see him again.
Even Sam won't call me.
Damini won't look me in the eye.
If this is what it means to love,
take it away.
I don't want it.
I don't want it—

I feel a cool hand on my skin,
and I wake up screaming.

Fear and Anger Collide

And rise like bile in my throat,
coursing through my veins
like white-hot ice.

'Who are you?' I nearly shriek
at the shimmering apparition of a man
bathed in moonlight before me.

This is a nightmare,
this is a dream,
it has to be!

Why else would a man
be inside my room
at night?

'What do you want with me?'
I cross my arms and pull my legs close,
press my face into my knees.

The figure opens its mouth
and says in a jasmine-dipped voice,
'My name is Shikhandi.'

Shikhandi

I know that name from the Mahabharata,
the version I found in the library.

He is Draupadi's mortal brother,
neither God nor Goddess.

Announced female at birth,
but always a man,

and one of the greatest warriors
any of our epics have ever known.

Still, even though I know him now,
I am shivering, and

my words tumble out, quick with emotion.
'I know who you are. And I already know your story.'

Shikhandi does not move. The moonlight reflects
off his night skin, a gentle smile on his lips.

'Good. Because that is not the story
I am here to tell.'

Now my anger ebbs slightly.
'Why not?'

'We do not come when we are called, child.
And you do not always get a mirror to reflect your pain.

We come to give you lessons.
Sometimes hard, sometimes unfair, but always needed.

And I am a little more human than divine.
It's why they sent *me* this time to you.'

I open my mouth to speak, and then close it again.
I remember what Nani has told me,

Listening is a superpower.
Not many possess it, but those that do it well

know how to go through life with more ease
than those of us who love the sound of our own voices.

He smiles, reading my mind, and says,
'Wise woman, your nani. Now. Here are the stories.'

The Fifth Stories

Love and prayer have a lot in common. They are both made from magic in many, many ways. When your love or your prayer is pure and heartfelt, the universe has no choice but to listen to you. There are those who will tell you that you must only love the people they choose for you. Remember these tales and know that they are wrong.

1.

The Lord Vishnu, Preserver of the universe, has taken masculine avatars and reincarnated onto this earth often. We have seen him reincarnate as Rama and Krishna, walk the Earth amongst humans and spirits alike, and brought justice with them wherever they went.

But what is not mentioned often enough is that the Lord Vishnu was not constricted to his male form. He had a feminine form, her name was Mohini. It was Mohini who enchanted men and Gods alike when she walked among them. Once, Shiva called to her to help him banish Bhasmasura, the ash demon, through her hypnotic dance. Once, she fell in love with Shiva and they had a child, the great teacher Maha Shastha.

If a God can embrace such different forms, who are mortals to tell other mortals they are less valid if they do?

2.

Agni, the God of Fire, was intense and striking. He is the one who brought Sita out from the flames, when Rama made her test her chastity – he was the ultimate test of purity, fire is also known to cleanse all it touches. He also believed in loving who he wanted to as he wanted to love them.

He was married to the goddess Svaha and he loved her endlessly. But one day, when walking through the forest, a wildfire of a God that he was, he looked up at the sky and fell in love with the full moon.

Raising his arms towards the sky, he begged the moon to come to him, begged the moon to love him back too.

Within moments, the moon became a beautiful God, with glittering silver hair, a serene smile and open arms, and they embraced. And Soma and Agni have been together ever since.

If two Gods can love each other with no objection from the divine or the universe, who are mortals to tell other mortals who they can and cannot love?

3.

Once there was a princess named Ratnavali. Her closest companion was the daughter of her king father's advisor, Brahmani. The two loved each other so much they could not bear the idea of being apart. So their fathers arranged their marriage in the same household, that of King Brihadbala.

Now this is where fate intervenes. Somewhere in the kingdom, a young man who needs a purification ritual comes begging at the king's door for the blessings of Ratnavali. When he looks upon her, she looks back at him like a mother does a son, and with the purity in her heart heals him.

Brihadbala refuses to let Ratnavali marry into his household as she, in his eyes, is now already a mother. So Ratnavali and Brahmani run away into the forest and live together, happily ever after.

If two women of legend and lore can find eternal love and happiness with each other, who are mortals to deny it to other mortals?

After the Fifth Story

Paro: I wish I wasn't different.

Shikhandi: There are things to wish for. That is not one of them.

Paro: Why? I feel like I have hurt everyone I love because I am different.

Shikhandi: No. You have not. This is why I told you these stories. That burden was never yours to carry. It belongs to those who are hurt by the idea that you are more than what they perceive you to be. You cannot hurt people by being who you are when it does not actually harm them in any way.

Paro: How do I fix it?

Shikhandi: There is absolutely nothing to fix. There is nothing broken about you.

Paro: I feel like I am shame and sadness and nothing more.

Shikhandi: But you are so much more. Be patient, child. All will come to you in time. You just need to get better at accepting love when it is given to you.

Paro: I'm afraid.

Shikhandi: We all are. If we had no fears to master, how else would we grow?

The Next Day

I am trembling when I walk into class.
Shikhandi's stories ring within my head.
I am still trying to make sense of them,
but my brain is so foggy with tears.

Mama didn't look at me this morning.
I didn't even see Papa
when I left for the bus stop.
At least I got a big hug from Indra.

My brother has always been good
at recognising sadness and replacing it
with happiness for people
before they even realise it.

Still, my heart thumps uncomfortably,
making my body feel like it is a tree
slowly being struck at by an axe.
Each thump makes me weaker,

and the classroom door feels
like it is a wood chipper waiting to end me.
I take a deep breath and square my shoulders,
push it open and

       walk straight into Mahi.

I Smile Despite Myself When I See Her

Quickly, I rummage into my bag
and hand her the poem.

'This is for you!'
The words tumble out in a rush.

'You said you wanted
to read my poetry. I wrote you this to say—'

I notice, too late,
that she is not alone.

Priya Snatches the Letter

And hands it over to Shalini,
who lets out a malicious giggle
and holds it out of my reach
as I try to take it back desperately.

I can feel eyes on us now,
other students watching the drama unfold.
I turn to Shalini, all wrath and knife-mouthed,
and say through gritted teeth:

'Give it back, *right now*!'

Shalini ignores me and opens the letter,
each crinkle of paper making my fists clench.
And in a loud, high-pitched, sing-song voice,
she reads out my apology.

Each syllable brings sniggers
from the people around us
and sets my teeth on edge.
I can't even look at Mahi.

Instead I squeeze my eyes shut
until the last words are out of Shalini's lips.
I love you – they sound so vile in her mocking tone,
bloated with venom, devoid of their intention.

You know that nightmare, where you are naked
and the whole class is pointing at you and laughing?
That's how I feel right now, with their hoots and hollers,
my whole body rigid as their insults lay bare my secret.

And then, Shalini's voice says nastily,
'So, Mahi, what do you say to Paro?'
She waves the note in her downcast face.
'Do you love her and her awful poetry too?'

Mahi pushes Shalini's arm out of her face.

'Don't be disgusting, Shalini.
Of course not.'

The force of the words hits me
like a poisonous snake bite,
and I stare at Mahi in shock.
She finally looks at me,

and for a split second,
I see my pearl-eyed Goddess,
but in the next second,
I see a cold, angry stranger.

Rage fills her face,
a hatred so hot in her eyes,
that I feel tears lodged heavily
keeping my voice locked in my throat.

She takes the poem from Shalini,
rips it up and throws it in my face.
The paper falls like forgotten leaves
all around me but I barely feel it.

'Leave me alone, you pervert.
I'm not unnatural like YOU.'

Bullet-shaped words
that go straight into my soul.
My eyes blur, and to my horror
I hear myself let out a loud sob.

Behind me, I hear the door,
and Mrs Krishnan's voice scolds,
'What is happening here?!
Paro, pick those pieces off the floor!'

The Difference Between Alone and Lonely

Alone has treated me kinder
than lonely ever could.
Alone is the comfort of libraries.
The solace of Audre Lorde's poetry.

Lonely is Mahi, who I once thought of as the world,
standing up in front of the whole class
and asking the teacher,
'Please, ma'am, can I change seats?'

Lonely is cruel like that.
It feels like a thousand eyes staring at me.
I think of Draupadi in court,
her eyes closed in prayer through indignity,

I do the same.
> Keep your head bowed,
> pray to every Goddess you know.

Alone directs your thoughts: *maybe if I run fast enough*
when the bell rings, I can get to the library
before the vultures fall upon me.
This is what lonely does. It makes you prey.

Maybe you can outrun your lonely,
I tell myself determinedly.
And when the bell rings,
I grab my things

and race down the corridors
before lonely can catch me.
I reach the doors of the library,
throw my shredded poem into the bin,

and promise myself in humiliated fury

I will NEVER write poetry again.

The Library

In the mythology section, I hide my face
in the big leather-bound copy of the Ramayana.
At first, it feels like I have beaten the tears back,
and I inhale a sigh of relief.

I think about the prince of Ayodhya, Rama,
reincarnation of the God Vishnu,
and his devoted brother Lakshmana
and his beloved wife Sita –

how they refuse to leave his side
even though he is not king any more,
even though the path ahead of him looks difficult.
And this is when the tears run down my face.

They run and splash, making the ink
streak on the yellowing page.
'Are you okay?' asks a quiet voice.
I turn around to see Sam's concerned face.

Sam Knows Everything

He tells me this as he sits next to me
and puts an arm around my shoulder.

'Why didn't you tell me you were gay?'

I close the book quietly.
'Because I'm not.'

'Paro.' His voice carries a sigh in it.
'I saw how Mahi and you looked at each other.'

'There are *other* things than gay,'
I snap with more annoyance than I mean to.

I am behaving like an injured animal,
but I don't know how to stop it.

His arm falls from my shoulder.
I instantly feel bad.

You need to accept love better,
Shikhandi had said.

I take a deep breath, inhale the smell
of musty books deeply, and cough.

'I'm sorry. I didn't mean to be rude.'
Sam looks away. 'S'okay.'

But it isn't.
I can tell it isn't.

'Is this why you've been avoiding me?'

I swallow hard. *Be honest and be brave with it.*
'Yes. It is.'

'Did you think I would hate you?
That I have room in my heart for hate,

after what our families went through?'
My face reddens with mortification.

Sam never brings up Kashmir
or partition. I always thought it was because

he wasn't as affected by it.
I was wrong.

Sometimes people don't mention pain
because they have known it too deeply.

'All those terrible things people did to each other
in the name of religion, and you think …

You think I would treat you that way
because you're different?'

The tears flow like deep rivers down my cheeks
and I hide my face. 'I'm sorry,' I whisper quietly.

He is silent.
Then wraps his arms around me

and lets me cry until his beige school-uniform shirt
is soaked through with salt water.

When I Come Back to Class

I find my bag dumped in the bin.
Someone has taken a ballpoint
and covered it in the words
bitch, freak, pervert,
monster

monster

monster

Sam picks it up from the bin.
I can't bring myself to.
He walks to the bathroom,
brings back paper towels
drenched
in water.

Together, we slowly try
to dissolve the ink,
like our grandparents
dissolved memories
to preserve their survival,
like the family they could not bury,
like the houses they watched burn,
like the grief they never healed from.

The ink fades
but you can still see traces.
Just like the scars that always remain.

After School

This used to be my favourite time of the day –
when the bus dropped me off at the dusty old bus stop.

And I would skip-walk home all the way
thinking of the book I borrowed from the library

or what I would draw in my sketchbook –
but today, my stomach hurts with anxiety.

So there is no skip-walking.
Mama opens the door and gives me a quick hug,

no kiss on the top of my head.
She's busy with Indra, I rationalise.

No need to think the worst.
Papa has gone into town for an errand.

Mama doesn't ask how school was today
when I join her and Indra at the table for some mangoes.

Indra says, 'Di, you know what I did today?'
His always happy face can't help but make me smile.

'What did you do?'
And as Indra tells me about his day,

I sneak a glance at my mother.
I know the way she is looking at me now.

It's how I looked at Mahi today.
Like she was suddenly a stranger.

That Night

Shikhandi visits again.
I look at his shimmering form,
all translucent in the moonlight,
like he is both myth and fairytale.

I tell him sadly, my voice breaking,
'I think I ruined everything.'
He says nothing.
Just walks over to me

and gives me
the kindest, warmest hug.

Today Is a Chance to Start Things Anew

And Mama is already at the table,
hands folded,
an empty placemat
before her.

I sit across from her,
but I do not touch my porridge.
She looks up at me,
dark circles under her eyes.

'Paro, Papa and I
think it's best for you to go
and stay at Nana Nani's house
for the summer.'

She doesn't say why but I know.
People are talking about me.
Passing comments to her
with spiteful glee.

When you are a teenage girl,
people see you less as a child, more as a bowl
where they place their expectations
and family reputation,
                        and demand you do not spill.

People talk
is how they keep us obedient.
People talk
is how they keep us silent and still.

'Paro, I do not want what happened
to A–' She pauses, reconsiders,
then speaks again, quietly, 'What happened
to our family friend's daughter happening to you.'

I swallow hard and ask,
my stomach aching with worry,
'But what happened to her?'

Mama's face darkens.

She takes a newspaper
and places it in front of me,
'This. THIS is what happens
when you behave the way you have.'

I stare at the paper

It says:

'Protestors storm cinema halls with lathis, beat audience members to protest film that depicts homosexuality. They call for the arrest of the director, cast and film crew.'

Black-and-white pictures of furious people
violently setting fire to posters
of two women laughing
and holding each other.

Threats of murdering
women who love women.
Words that say women like me
destroy families and countries.

I drop the paper
like it has burned my fingers
and sit back
wide-eyed in fear.

My mother looks at me,
sadness in her eyes. 'You see?
I just want you to be safe,
my baby. They do *this* to people too.'

I say nothing, but nod.
I must know which battles to pick
if I am to live through all of this.

Besides, my grandmother's house
is my favourite place in the world.
Even so, I feel no bliss.

Nani's House

It has been a long time since I visited Paradise.
But Paradise has not forgotten about me.
My old friend the sun climbs in through
the upstairs window, spilling all over
the smooth stone floors,
all the way across the ancient green carpet
till it settles across my face, and I open my eyes.
The anxiety doesn't make my stomach hurt
as I slowly get up and rub my eyes.
There is something about Kashmiri air
that lightens all burdens.
I can hear the myna birds sing
from the old banyan trees in the gardens.
The cows are mooing from the nearby field.
I slip on my chappals and go to the bathroom,
and my reflection smiles happily back at me.
There is no internet or computer here,
but there are books and a garden
and sketchbooks and paints,
and stories and love from my grandparents.

How fortunate am I
that even in exile,
I get to be in Paradise.

How fortunate am I
to still have grandparents who love me
unconditionally, no matter what I have done.

Breakfast with Nana-Nani

My grandmother is the most sacred person I know.
She wakes every morning before the roosters, even the crows

just to make herself and my grandfather
a piping hot cup of chai each. She says *love grows*

if you drink tea together every morning, and I believe her.
I have never seen two people more in love.

Not even my own parents.
When I have bathed, I join them downstairs

at the old mahogany dining table for breakfast.
The stairs of the old house creak as I bound down them.

'Good morning!' I say brightly, pressing a kiss
to my nana and then my nani's cheeks.

My nana's loud, infectious laugh fills the room,
as everything I do is a joy-filled moment to him.

My nani passes me the hard-boiled eggs and asks,
'How did you sleep, my dil ki tukdi?'

And I can honestly say while taking an egg,
'The best I've slept in years, my nani.'

Nana Papa's Tale

Now in the garden,
with the mosquito repellent
slathered on our legs,
and the fireflies floating close by
on the old swing in the verandah,
Nana tells me stories
from his childhood.

He tells me about Dal Lake.
How the water reflected the blue of the sky,
and on a still day you could make clouds ripple
through the water with a stone.
What growing up on a houseboat was like.
How the waters rocked him to sleep every night.

And then, when he was seventeen,
the men came with swords.
They brought butchery
and bloodshed with each footstep.

They told my great-grandfather
if he didn't leave, they would take his wife,
his daughters, and kill his sons.

So my great-grandparents
filled the old jeep
with what they could.

Just as they were about to leave,
a father came begging for help for his daughter.
But there was only enough room for one.
So my grandfather got out without a word,
and gave his seat to the father and daughter.

'My family wept and wept.
Told me not to do it.
I did it anyway.'

He winces. The arthritis bites into his knees
as he tries to stand up. I move to help him,
but he shakes his head. So instead I ask,

'Why did you do it, Nana Papa?'

He looks me straight in the eyes;
even in the dying light I can see them glimmer.

'How could I live with myself
knowing I had separated that girl
from her only living parent,
while my whole family survived?'

I am quiet as I digest this slowly.
'But how did you know you would
all make it through alive?'

He takes my hand and squeezes it.

'I didn't. I just knew what kind of man
I wanted to be if I did make it out alive.'

The Next Morning

I wake up to the ding of a message
coming through on my phone.

I rub the sleep from my eyes as I lift it,
disconnect it from its charger.

It's hard for messages to come through here.
Even phone calls crackle so close to the border.

I assume it's my mother, or my father, or even Sam,
until the name on the screen makes my stomach drop.

Mahi.

I swallow hard, close my eyes,
and try to still my racing heart

before I look back at the screen.
My thumb hovers over the button to open it,

and then, after a deep, steadying breath,
I do.

'**Hi Paro.**
I am sorry for how I acted in school.
I shouldn't have done that to you.
My parents are religious,
and they were so angry at me.
They told me if I ever
did something like that again
they would disown me.
And Shalini and Priya
would have made fun of me too.
I'm not like you, Paro.
I'm not okay being on the outside.
I can't handle being laughed at,
the way they laugh at you.

I need my friends, they make me feel safe,
like I am one of them.
Besides, you know what they do
to people like us here.
I promise I won't ever hurt you again.
Can we go back to being friends?'

My hand squeezes
the phone tighter
with each word I read until
my fingertips are white
from strain.

Fury makes its way through my body.
I slam the phone down on my bed
and go to get ready for my day.
But when I look at myself
in the bathroom mirror, I am shaking.

A hundred thousand excuses.
That is all I see in her message.
Not an apology,
but a demand
for forgiveness.

In that moment I see
Mahi as a villain
who is happy to throw me
to the wolves,
just to save her own skin.

The House Temple

Nani knows something is wrong
from the minute I set foot downstairs.

I do not join in their conversation;
instead I stew over Mahi's inconsideration.

I pick at an apple, finishing it only
because I know Nani doesn't like waste.

But before I can skulk away from the table,
I hear her say, 'Paro, come with me.'

I sigh and grudgingly go with her.
She takes me to the temple inside the house.

We fold our hands in prayer,
and she says the Gayatri mantra.

When she finishes the hymn,
I notice she has a crimson scarf in her hands.

She slowly pulls apart the crimson scarf
and pulls out a pack of large indigo-blue cards.

'This,' she says quietly,
'belonged to your great-grandmother.

It is a gift of sight and clarity
called the Tarot.'

The Cards

Nani shows me the cards.
Beautiful ancient illustrations
cover their yellowing surfaces
from edge to edge.

She shows me what they are.
Major arcanas, court cards,
wands, swords,
pentacles, cups.

She tells me about the gift
all the women in my family hold
but no one ever talks about.
Not even my own mother.

'This is why she sent you here,'
says my grandmother.
'She discovered her own gift
when she was your age.'

And I, in all my childishness ask,
'Is it witchcraft?'
That earns me a light smack
on the side of my head.

'Don't be ridiculous, girl.
The cards are a sacred gift
from the Goddess herself.
Anything that people don't understand,

they give labels so it's easier to fear.
They do this to all things unusual.
The Goddesses themselves will tell you.'

That Night

I lay the cards before me,
close my eyes, and say a prayer

to every Goddess and God,
the universe itself, and Shikhandi too.

I ask them to wrap their protection
around me. Then I ask the cards quietly,

'Tell me. What should I say to Mahi?'
I shuffle and gradually my answers fall out.

First, The Magician:
I am the master of my own manifestation.

Second, Ace of Swords:
A severance will bring new beginnings.

Third, The World:
All cycles must come to completion.

I take a deep breath,
and count to ten.

Then I say thank you
to all who are watching over me.

I carefully put the cards back into
their crimson and gold scarf

and tuck them under my pillow.
Slowly, I type these words on the screen.

**'I am sorry the only way you feel in control
is when you are in a group inflicting pain.**

There is a difference
between power and powerful.

When you have power,
you can hurt someone with it,

but powerful is when you help someone in trouble,
even if you don't benefit.

I forgive you, Mahi.
But I don't know if I will trust you ever again.'

I press *send*, and sigh deeply.
It feels like a weight has lifted from me.

But one thing she said to me stays with me,
even as I close my eyes.

'*You know what they do to people like us.*'

I know this is Paradise for me,
but I cannot stay here hiding for ever.
Eventually I will have to go back.

Back to Mama's hurting heart.
Back to classmates jeering at me.
Back to where I cannot be me.

Maybe if I go far away from here,
I'll find a place where I can just be.
As I drift off to sleep I think,

'If they cannot have me for who I am
then maybe here is not
where I am meant to be.'

Naareetv

Womanhood

Even the day must let go of the sun
and allow the light to disappear,
so the darkness can live for a while.

The only way out of grief is through it.
How else does one make way for dawns,
and new beginnings where healing smiles?

A New City

All big cities look alike somehow.
The food changes, the language changes,
the people change.

And yet everything remains the same.
Whether you call it a metro or the underground.
Whether you name it Chandni Chowk or Hackney.

All cities are siblings,
and I picture them sitting at a table,
Sunday afternoon with the family.

Paris dressed in white Chanel
sipping Chardonnay, smoking a cigarette,
arguing with—

Rome, dark eyes glittering with mischief,
historical innuendos about Nero and Caesar,
sitting next to—

Kingston, gently smiling, old camera in hand,
taking photos while discussing music, dance
and architecture with—

Tokyo, all soft cherry blossoms and a gentle way,
a love of history and art and how they show up
in monuments, which is why—

My now beloved Delhi is keenly adding
to this conversation, wearing a pristine saree,
glorious in her splendour while—

Copenhagen and New York squabble playfully,
Cairo and Nassau engage in deep conversation
and—

And then there is London, mysterious,
watching the fireplace, aloof, sometimes cold.
But *always* with a story to tell.

'Miss Madera.' I look up from my reverie
at the unsmiling immigration officer.
He pronounces it *mad-error*.

I am about to correct him,
but he is already waving the next person through
and I am staring at a sign that says,

'Welcome to London.'

London

The Piccadilly Line is full,
but the only people speaking
are the young Spanish couple
sitting next to me.

As the train rocks away
to its destination,
I try to look at the people around me
without staring like I am brand new.

'Don't look like prey,'
my father warned me before I left.
And I had nodded quietly,
knowing what he was trying to say.

Young women alone are easy to mark.
This may not be Delhi,
but girls go missing here too.
I don't think cities mean to be dangerous

but some crueler people can't help themselves,
so I busy myself with a book,
try to look like just another eighteen-year-old bored,
try to look like someone self-assured.

The train halts at King's Cross
and as I exit the doors
I wonder if I had managed it –
mastered the art of being invisible

                of making myself look like unprey.

Mama Barely Spoke to Me Before I Left

She wanted me to go to university in Delhi.
But when I was sixteen, my mind was made up.
So I worked, and I studied, and I did everything I could
until between Papa and Nani and a bursary,

I could finally come to university here.
A place so far away from home
I could truly explore who I needed to be.
A place where I *thought* they wouldn't hurt me for being me.

She told me, 'I think you will find London
is not the dream you believe it to be.'
And when I asked her why, she simply said,
'Just take care of your soft heart, my baby.'

Art School

Standing outside the university building
that looks more like an old English boarding school,

old heavy double doors with large ornate handles,
white statues that simultaneously seem welcoming

and intimidating, I take a shaky breath and close my eyes.
I try to picture what Shikhandi or Draupadi

or Shashthi or Lakshmi would do at a time like this.
As if the cold September wind herself knows what
I am asking,

she whispers the answer into my slowly numbing ears,
'They would embrace their fortune and go within.'

International Students

The hall is so crowded.
Tables border the walls
labelled with the course names,
tired soon-to-be students line up with bags
to find out where to go next.

We are here earlier than the local students
so we can settle in after our long flights.
I follow the signs to the Illustration table;
a smiling lady in a blue cardigan and big glasses
hands me a massive pack of papers.

'These are the directions to your accommodation,
your schedule, places to eat outside of halls,
counselling offices, administration buildings,
important phone numbers,'
she rattles off so quickly I can barely keep up.

I smile and nod anyway.
I'm sure I can figure it out.
I don't want to ask too many questions
and seem like I am ignorant or a burden,
or even worse, just not listening.

I look around at the other international students
wondering if any of them are headed
to the same accommodation as me.
I don't want to get lost
but mostly,

I would like the chance
to turn a stranger into a friend.

'Are You Lost?'

Asks a deep, friendly voice.
Definitely English, I think,
as I turn around with a big smile on my face.
Instantly, I wish I had brushed my teeth
after the eight-hour plane journey.

Curly dark hair falls into his eyes
and a crooked smile rests on his face.
He's wearing a white shirt
and a badge that says *Student Help*,
along with the name *Devon*.

His skin is olive like mine,
and he walks in it with such ease.
Two pretty girls walk past us
and he nods at them, sending them giggling.
I think, *why is everyone here out of my league?*

'Are you lost?'
he repeats,
slower this time,
probably thinking
I may not speak English.

I nod slightly. He raises an eyebrow,
and I realise I am staring.
I look down at my feet awkwardly.
'Um, I'm supposed to go to Tooting?'
He winces dramatically.

'Wow, they put you far away for a first year.'
I seize the opportunity for a joke.
'Yeah, it's because I'm poor.'
He tilts his head and grins.
'I think you're a lot better off than most.'

And I blush, because he is right.
I don't mean to sound spoilt and ungrateful.
He gestures to my folder, 'Let me help you.'
I give it to him and he clicks his pen.
He pulls out the TFL map and marks the route.

My eyes follow his hand
so that I don't stare at his face
and the intensity of his hypnotic eyes.
Something about him felt so familiar.
I shook the feeling off, it was just jetlag brain, surely.

He clicked his pen and showed me the map.
'This is going to be your Bible.
Take these three trains,
and you should be there in an hour.'
I take it back appreciatively. 'Thank you.'

He grins again. 'No worries.
I'll see you there sometime.
I live around there too.'

And despite myself, this makes my stomach flutter
in a way it hasn't in a long, long time.
Not since Mahi.

Halls

I am the only person in my flat,
and will be for a whole day.
Honestly, I'm glad for it.
The place seems big but only
because eight of us must share it.

My tiny room is almost perfect.
There is a desk and a chair
for when I want to work,
a bulletin board to plan my days,
and a view of the student village
from my window.

The only thing that I struggle with
is the bed. My feet hang over the edge
when I try to lie down
on the fresh sheets I bought
from the Sainsbury's nearby.

I pick up my phone and switch the SIM,
to 1p per minute international calls,
then quickly dial Indra,
'Hi, I'm in Halls now.'
His voice sounds so very far away as he says,

'That's great! How are you settling in, di?'
And a lump in my throat.
I say, 'It's great.
I'm settling in fine.'
But all I can think is,

It's going to be so many months
before I see you again, bhai.

Ratri

I wake up in the darkness.
I didn't even realise I had fallen asleep
talking to Indra, phone still clutched
in my hand.

Someone is here.
Right here in this room with me.
I see the shape in the darkness
by the wardrobe.

It strikes me in that moment,
I've never really been alone somewhere at night before.
Mama, Papa, Indra, Damini, Nana, Nani,
someone has always been there to call on.

You learn to take safety for granted
if it is always there.
And now … I am alone in an empty flat,
with something staring at me.

I start to shake as I raise my phone,
about to switch on the torch,
but a voice fills the dark room.
'You have nothing to fear.

I am the Devi
of love and the night.
I think you know
why I am here.'

The Sixth Story

I was born in darkness. Long before the old Gods or the newer Gods or golden forest, this universe was nothing but abyss. My mother was divine creator to all of this – the Devi herself. For a long time she floated unaware of herself. Unaware of the world around her. And because she grew lonely, being the only one here, she wished for a child and manifested me.

There in the darkness, my mother's face shone like a galaxy, and it is the first memory I ever had. Long before I wore nebulae as anklets and opened my third eye.

They call me many names. The Greeks called me Nyx. But my mother named me Ratri, meaning Night. And I grew up dancing stars into existence, making my mother smile so she crafted me a brand new moon, writing alive the Trimurti alongside her.

We were the First Ones. Divine feminine energy that nurtured everything around us alive. But the idea of a mother and daughter writing an everlasting poem together called the universe, bringing male energy into existence, didn't suit the people who told this story. So slowly, we were erased out of it. Put aside for a more palatable story.

The Devi, my mother is both Balance and Chaos. She is the beginning and end of all things. I too come from the same divine blood.

The Trimurti – Shiva, Vishnu and Brahma – knew this. No one ever challenged me, the night. I was unlimited power, walking across the universe in my veil, bringing darkness wherever I went.

When my sister Ushas was born, I could not have been happier. This was our family of darkness and balance. My mother, my sister and me.

And then … Surya, the sun and the light, was brought into the world. From the moment he was born, he was relentless – his light was so bright, it was painful for my darkness. Wherever I went, he chased me, and I was not allowed to use my powers to stop him, for I could easily turn him to dust. My mother, who maintained balance across the universe, would not allow this. If his rays ever touched me directly, they would burn my skin. Instead, I had to learn to leave every time he was near, giving him time to shine. The days grew longer and the nights grew shorter till I could barely give my planets an hour. His very presence made me unhappy, because it meant I would have to run. My sister Ushas sensed this. We were so close, she always knew when I was in pain and I always knew when she was too.

She asked me one day, 'I cannot see you in pain any more. Please tell me how do I help you?'

I sighed as I sat back, waiting for Surya to set. 'You cannot, Ushas, no one can. He must make the choice.' And I glared in the direction of the sun from the place where I stayed in wait.

Ushas smiled at me, 'Di, if he bothers you that much, I'll find a way to make him stop.'

I saw them as words of comfort. The gentle ways between sisters. I never thought she was going to do what she did.

Ushas met him. Surya. Despite the anguish the force of his abrasive light caused her, she walked into his celestial palace in Devlok and asked to meet him. He was charting his pathways across the universe at the time. Trying to find a way to completely eradicate me. Make me extinct.

This made Ushas furious. She demanded, 'What will it take to make you leave my sister alone?'

And Surya, who was smitten with both the might and beauty of this primordial Goddess said, almost in a trance, 'You. It will take you being my bride and walking before me.'

'Impossible. Ancient Ones cannot live in Devlok, you know this as well as me. And you are the kind of light our family of darkness cannot be around for you burn everything that you touch. Even being here is agony for me.'

Surya, who was a born negotiator, brought her amrit, and handed it to her to drink. 'If you drink this, you will be able to live with me, and I will relent: let your sister fly free for an equal half of my time. But there is a caveat,' he added.

Ushas looked up at him, waiting.

'If you drink this, you will never be able to see your sister again. Not the way you did before.'

'But she will be safe and you won't chase her into exile any more?'

He put a hand to his chest and bowed slightly. 'You have my word.'

My sister loved me so much she made the choice within a heart-beat. She drank from the cup and let the light burn within her until … until she was no longer darkness, but the rosy fingers of dawn and twilight.

She is known as the ease into the day, and the ease into the night.

She became his bride so I, the night, could run free. She walks before him, a reincarnated Goddess of Dawn and Twilight, so that the burn of his rays cannot ever hurt me. In the end, it was not power, but my sister's sacrifice that brought me liberty.

I Am Older Now

I am no longer the child the Goddesses used to visit.
Too old to believe in fairytales
or that myths are talking to me.

Why would they?
I'm not that special anyway.
I've spent a great deal of time explaining all of that away.

Trauma made me imagine my books into existence.
The need to be accepted made me turn to religion.
All children had imaginary friends; mine were the Goddesses.

There was a rational explanation
for why they visited me
and it was because they weren't at all.

So this, now, feels like a dream.
It has to be. I've spent so much time
unbreaking what I thought was a broken mind.

Surely this is nothing but a dream,
a story I read somewhere,
a book from my childhood.

But nothing can change the fact
that my eyes clearly
saw a night-skinned woman dressed in a black saree,

slowly weaving small nebulae
into her hair sitting
at the end of my bed.

After the Sixth Story

Paro: I thought—

Ratri: You thought you had outgrown us and imagined us. Yes. They said this is what you had done.

Paro: I'm too old for imaginary friends.

Ratri: Perhaps we are not too old for you, girl. In the grand scheme of the universe, death only comes for one of us. And I've been here from the beginning of time itself. You are more imaginary than I could ever be.

Paro: Why does no one else see you then? Why do people not know you exist? Why do they question the Gods and the Goddesses if they are right there?

Ratri: You don't see the wind either. But you do know it is there. You know it exists. You feel it. Faith works the same way.

Paro: So is it all just a test?

Ratri: Everything is a test; it is how you evolve into what you are meant to be. The same rules apply to mortals and immortals alike.

Paro: About your sister. Did she ever grow to love him?

Ratri: We are good at adapting, women and Goddesses alike.

Paro: Why did you tell me that story? I have no sisters.

Ratri: Maybe it is time you found some.

I Don't Sleep the Rest of the Night

Instead, I lie in bed and wonder
why a Goddess would visit me.
I raise my arm and pinch my skin
till it is bruised to make sure I am awake.

I wonder if my mind
is playing tricks on me.
If there is something
wrong with me.

Maybe this is a side effect
of depression or trauma
or anxiety?
But in my heart I know what I saw.

I know she was there.
In my campus room,
so ancient that she did not look
out of place at all.

Like the sky,
the stars,
the sea,
or the wolf's call.

By the time
the sun comes out,
I have only just closed
my eyes to sleep.

The Streets of Tooting

I do what I know all my heroes did
when they were lost in thought.

I pack a tote with a sketchbook and pencils
and I go for a long, meandering walk.

Walks with no destination
are a powerful source of inspiration.

A good way to make sense of something
that makes no sense at all.

So I walk through the student village,
a strange thing to call it

given that it was just buildings
facing a pretty courtyard

with a large garden in the centre.
Already, I see a few people collecting there,

laughing, joking, getting to know each other.
I keep walking, towards what is called the high street.

I am determined to get to know Tooting better.
I come across a closed kebab shop on my way,

a few more places offering 'takeaway'.
All the banks collect ominously

in one part of this busy street,
looking like men in suits in a business meeting.

I laugh to myself, thinking,
I can't wait to tell my family.

Then pause, remembering how far away they are.
And a phone call just doesn't do it justice.

Instantly I reprimand myself
for feeling any kind of self-pity.

'You chose to be here, Paro.
This was your decision.'

I shove the pain deep down,
square my shoulders, and keep walking.

As soon as I start walking again,
I hear someone yell,

'Hey! HEY!' and I turn around to see
Devon running across the road to me.

I try to ignore how my heart skips a beat.
He reaches me, slightly out of breath,

and says, 'You walk fast! Remember me?'
How could anyone not?

I say, 'Yes, I do. Hi.'
I can tell he's been running,

he has blue running shoes on
and sweat dots his brow

and darkens his blue t-shirt.
It makes me less conscious

that I'm in old comfortable sweats
and a jumper,

He looks at his watch,
'You're up early.'

'Couldn't sleep.'
The words tumble out before I can stop them.

He tilts his head, looking at me curiously.
'Want to talk about it? I know a coffee place.'

'Um … okay,'
I hear myself say.

This has never happened to me before,
so why not see where it goes?

One thing is for sure,
I'm not in Delhi any more.

Devon

He's from East London.
He says this like it means
a whole lot to him,

and I can't help but smile.
People are most exquisite
when they talk about what they love.

He's a second year in Fine Art
and he really loves chocolate.
I know because he's eating a chocolate muffin

and drinking a mocha.
His hazel eyes
have enough warm brown in them

to remind me of the old banyan
in Nani's garden right after a storm.
And he seems to never run out

of things to say.
I know everything about him
within fifteen minutes,

from his zodiac sign (Gemini)
to his mother's name (Anita),
how his mother is Indian

and his father is English.
How they named him Devon
because his mother preferred Dev

but his father wanted Simon.
It is deeply comforting to speak
with someone so open.

There is no pressure to dance
around a conversation.
'Sorry,' he says, looking embarrassed.

'I talk a lot.'
I cradle my latte, leaning back.
'Don't apologise. It's nice. I like listening.'

He shakes his head.
'I haven't even asked
what you're studying at uni.'

I smile. 'It's illustration.'
Truth be told I'm worried.
I'm not sure if I'm any good.

Almost like he can hear my thoughts he says,
'You must be good to get into uni.
They have a very selective course.'

I look at my latte,
ever uncomfortable
with compliments.

'Tell me, Paro.'
The way he speaks my name
makes me feel as soft as a good dream.

'Why couldn't you sleep?'

The Truth

Is always deeply complicated.
I don't know how to share it with family,
let alone someone I've only just met.

I am full of secrets I cannot share with anyone;
the only places I can give them away
are within the drawings now that I don't write poetry.

Who would believe Goddesses visit me?
Who would believe what happened in the bazaar?
I've seen on TV and in the news

how people treat women who come forward.
We are called liars and troublemakers,
besmirched with wretched reputations ever after.

So I take a deep breath and say,
'I just have nightmares sometimes.'
And quickly change the subject back to him.

Devon Has To Leave For Class Soon

But before he goes, he says,
'I could talk to you forever.'
And despite myself,

a blush rises to my cheeks.
My heart beats a little quicker
as he smiles from the door and waves at me.

I look around the little café.
There are only four tables,
and I've got the one by the window.

It makes for good people-watching.
Mothers push babies past in prams,
and sleepy people grab their coffees before work.

I feel a bit embarrassed
at not having something to do
while everyone else is being productive

so I pull out my sketchbook and 4B pencil.
In my mind's eye, Ratri and Ushas come alive,
and I sketch them dancing across the cosmos.

Find sisters, Ratri had said.
I look up to watch as two girls across the street
walk into a supermarket arm in arm, laughing.

As if it is so easy.

I Don't Know What I'm Doing Here

I just know that the flyer said *Desi Community*,
so here I am. It's just a classroom at the uni.
But somehow, with all these people in it,
it seems entirely otherworldly.

The chairs are arranged in a circle,
but no one is sitting in them.
People are in groups, laughing and talking.
I square my shoulders slightly and think,

'Okay, Paro, be brave. Go and make friends.'
But my feet won't move.
What if they stop talking when I approach?
I don't want to make people feel awkward.

As I debate my next move, a green-eyed girl
melts away from a group and walks over to me.
'Hey.' The way she speaks is bright and kind.
'My name is Sakshi. First year?'

'Hello, I'm Paro. Yes, I'm a first year.'
Sakshi's beautiful face brightens.
'Oh, you're from India!
So pleased you found us.'

This strikes me as odd.
Isn't everyone here from India?
And then I realise,
she means, all of them grew up here.

She means, I am the same in a different way.
I guess she heard it in my accent.
I feel a little uncomfortable suddenly,
like I'm the odd one out.

It doesn't help that all the people here
look like Apsaras, Devis and Devas
straight out of *Amar Chritra Katha*.
They're all perfect, well dressed,
Goddess and God confidence, and I am … well, me.

Sakshi must have noticed me fretting
because she says, 'Don't worry, lovely.
Everyone here is really nice.'
She puts an arm through mine and says,

'Why don't you just try and give it a chance?'

The Invitation

She's right. Everyone here IS nice.
This is desi hospitality at its best;
you can't help but be put at ease
by the jokes and warmth.

Delhi is heavily influenced
by the North Indian culture
that cradles it, but here
everyone has roots everywhere.

Kind of like a Kashmiri girl
from Delhi in London.
I hear Ratri's voice in my head.
It startles me, but I don't let it show.

Ali, the boy standing next to me, says,
'Where in Kashmir are you from?'
It's a question I wasn't expecting.
'Srinagar.' Every time I say it,

it almost feels like
it doesn't belong to me any more.
That was another girl. Another life.
'Ah, it's a beautiful place. Do you have family there?' he asks.
I nod, 'All my grandparents. Have you been?'

I don't say, I only visit my mother's parents.
My father's parents aren't in my life anymore.
They don't like us because we wouldn't
join in with their bigotry.

It still feels strange when people
talk to me about Kashmir.
Like I am pulled back into history class,
all those years ago.

To be Kashmiri is to walk a minefield
of other people's feelings
you never asked to walk
yet will always be there.

I brace myself for the strong opinions
I'm used to hearing from people
who have never lived there. They never come.
Instead he just says, 'Never. But I'd love to go.'

I beam, feeling at ease again,
and silly for being judgmental.
'You should. You would love it,
but it will also make you sad.'

'Because of all the trouble?'
He takes a sip of his Coke
and looks at me knowingly. I nod.
'Because of all the trouble.'

We leave it there and I am relieved.
But we talk about other things,
and it is eight o'clock in no time.
Three hours pass so quickly.

Before I leave, Sakshi presses an invite
into my hands and gives me a huge hug.
It surprises me when I hug her back.
'Make sure you come,' she says and disappears.

I look at the orange and yellow invite.
It says in black Devanagari-style lettering,
Diwali Party.
I can't stop smiling all the way to the library.

'Oi, Paki!'

The word assaults my ears
and stops me cold.
It feels like I'm in a movie,
because this cannot be real life.

Surely no one in London of all places
uses that word. *That* terrible, *cruel* word.
Especially not here, in Tooting,
so many South Asians live here.

My heart thuds as I walk faster.
I can hear them behind me.
It's the laughter that terrifies me.
It sounds like it comes from fang-filled mouths.

It's so dark.
Everything is closed.
No one else is out on the street,
and I am being followed.

I feel so foolish.
Why did I stay so late at the library?
Why didn't I just come home at eight
after hanging out with the community?

I am about to break into a run
when I feel someone yank me back
by my backpack and I stumble,
falling hard backwards on the pavement.

Pain shoots through my legs
and back, but the terror in me
has numbed me as I realise
I am now at their mercy.

A group of white boys circle me like sharks;
I can smell the alcohol and rage on them.
'Oi, Paki, why are you here?'
asks one, his words so slurred

I can barely make out what he is saying.
My heart is throbbing so hard in my ears,
Are they going to kill me?
'Please let me go.'

I can barely hear myself speak.
'Why don't you lot just go back?'
asks another boy, kicking at my thigh disgustedly,
I swallow my yelp into my throat.

He laughs cruelly then asks,
'What's in the bag?'
I grab it and pull it close,
but this is a mistake.

He rips it from my arms
and unzips it, letting my pencils
and sketchpad all clatter to the ground.
His big hand riffles through its pockets

and finds my wallet.
He chucks my bag and kneels;
his cold blue eyes send
icy shivers down my spine.

'Give me your phone.'
I shake my head hard.
My one link to my family,
I can't, I just can't—

'NOW.'

He reaches out to grab me
but I scramble back
and he misses, slipping comically
and making his friends snigger.

His demeanour shifts instantly
into intense rage as he roars,

'Paki BITCH,'

and lunges for me. I pull my knees
in tight and close my eyes

and wait for worse
than the bazaar,
wait for worse
than the fruit seller's hands

but … it never happens.
Instead I open my eyes
to see them running down the street
as if a shadow is chasing them.

I don't stop to find out why.
Instead I get up as fast as I can

and run

and run

and run

and don't stop
until I am inside my flat.

I realise others have moved in
in the time I have been gone.
All of the lights are on.

Before anyone can see me
I rush into my room,
lock the door,

and collapse
in a crumpled, messy heap
on the floor.

Terror

I can't believe this happened to me I can't believe this happened to me
I can't believe this happened to me I can't believe this happened to me
I can't believe this happened to me I can't believe this happened to me
I can't believe this happened to me I can't believe this happened to me
I can't believe this happened to me I can't believe this happened to me
I can't believe this happened to me I can't believe this happened to me
I can't believe this happened to me I can't believe this happened to me
I can't believe this happened to me I can't believe this happened to me
I can't believe this happened to me I can't believe this happened to me
I can't believe this happened to me I can't believe this happened to me
I can't believe this happened to me I can't believe this happened to me
I can't believe this happened to me I can't believe this happened to me
I can't believe this happened to me I can't believe this happened to me
I can't believe this happened to me I can't believe this happened to me
I can't believe this happened to me I can't believe this happened to me
I can't believe this happened to me I can't believe this happened to me
I can't believe this happened to me I can't believe this happened to me
I can't believe this happened to me I can't believe this happened to me
I can't believe this happened to me I can't believe this happened to me
I can't believe this happened to me I can't believe this happened to me
I can't believe this happened to me I can't believe this happened to me
I can't believe this happened to me I can't believe this happened to me
I can't believe this happened to me I can't believe this happened to me
I can't believe this happened to me I can't believe this happened to me
I can't believe this happened to me I can't believe this happened to me
I can't believe this happened to me I can't believe this happened to me
I can't believe this happened to me I can't believe this happened to me I
can't believe **this happened to me I can't believe
this happened to me I can't believe this
happened to me**

I Finally Breathed

As I sat up on my bedroom floor
and took stock of my situation.
Calmed myself by thinking,
I am not hurt. Not physically, at least.
There wasn't much in my wallet.
I left my bank card locked in my room.
Twenty pounds. An Oyster card.
But I felt awful for losing it.
Papa's hard-earned money.
A gift from Nani's savings.
It wasn't just mine to lose.
It wasn't just my hard work
that brought me here.
That was all the money
I had budgeted for food
and travel for the week.
I couldn't possibly call home
and ask for more,
I knew my parents didn't have it.
Now I didn't know what to do.
Still I couldn't help but think,
it could have been worse.

I didn't sleep that night either.
Just sat on my bed,
clutching my Tarot cards to my chest.
Every noise that came through the dark
made me jump out of my skin.

I Have My First Class This Morning

But I don't want to attend it.
I am far too frightened to leave my room.

I pick up my phone wanting to call my parents.
Wanting to speak to Indra.

And then I think, all that will do
is cause an ocean of worry

that would eventually end up
drowning me and all I wanted to do.

Mama will say, 'I told you so.'
Papa will say, 'Maybe this was a bad idea.'

What if they asked me to come back
and told Nani, who would persuade me to?

Imagine if Lakshmibai, Rani of Jhansi,
had given up before the rebellion began.

Imagine if Sarojini Naidu had given up the freedom struggle
because someone called her racist names.

Imagine how ashamed I would be of myself
if I gave up now.

So, instead, I put my phone down,
swallow back my tears and my fears,

and in a cocktail made of confidence and bravery,
leave my bed to get ready for the day.

I Take the Bus Instead of the Tube

It's cheaper.
I think of how I can budget
ten quid for this week
out of the twenty quid next week
for food.

It shouldn't be hard.
I'll just go to Asda.
Buy porridge and milk
and apples and baked beans.
A loaf of bread and eggs.

That should last me the week
if I'm careful enough.
I think of telling someone
what happened to me.
Maybe campus security?

I should. I should tell them,
so that no other students get hurt.
Feeling better and more in control,
I breathe a bit easier,
watch the rain fall across the city,

my head pressed against
the cool glass of the bus window.

Hit by a Freight Train

The first session is an introduction,
and I find it difficult to focus.
Two nights of sleeplessness
have returned to haunt me,
and I keep dozing off.

'Are you okay?' a soft voice asks.
'You look like you've been hit
by a freight train.' And despite myself,
I laugh. I look at the owner of the voice.
She has warm, luminous eyes,

long, lustrous black hair, and is in a loose
baby-blue jumper, skinny jeans and sneakers.
'I'm fine,' I answer when I find my voice.
'Didn't sleep much.'
She leans forward and whispers,

'Was it for good reasons?'
She raises her flawless arched eyebrows.
I chuckle again. 'I wish. I'm quite boring really.'
She beams, revealing
a cheeky, pretty dimple in her right cheek.

'Don't worry. There's always time.'
I cackle now, getting the lecturer's attention.
'Quiet please, pay attention,'
he says in annoyance.
We duck our heads and muffle our giggles.

After, as we are collecting our things
she introduces herself, 'I'm Joy.'
'Paro.' I offer my hand
and we grin at each other
and shake as if we already have a secret.

'Are you in the illustration course too?'
I nod and show her my schedule.
She squints at it, and points.
'I think we have the next class together.
Let's go wind up that lecturer too.'

Joy

Is every bit as delightful as her name suggests.
She's the kind of person who walks in
and brings sunshine with her
into the rooms that need it most.
Her sketchbook is filled with
incredibly lifelike pen and ink portraits,
so refined and detailed.

'I can't believe you're a first year.
You have the skills of
a grand master,'
I say to her in absolute awe
as I flip through her sketchbook
outside the class. She teases.
'Bet you say that to all the girls.'

I blush. Can she tell I'm bi?
But she has already moved on.
'Let's see your book.'
I wince. 'No way. Not after
seeing how good you are.'
She takes it from my open bag,
I shriek playfully, as she holds it
out of reach.

'Come on, let's see!'
She opens it up to see
the Tarot card illustrations
I've been making.
I cringe inwardly,
seeing every flaw in high-res detail.
'I'm not very good.
Not as good as you anyway.'

'Stop that,' she shushes my whining.
'Don't ever compare yourself.'
She turns and looks right in my eyes.
'Comparison is a form of violence
against yourself. Do you hear me?'
Her words ring so true
I instantly feel myself nodding.

'Good.' She beams.
'I won't be hearing any of that
if we are to be friends.'

The Witch's Arms,

As it is serendipitously named,
is the pub where Joy's best friend works.
And even though I say I can't
because I have no money,
Joy says she will buy me a rum and Coke,
especially after she finds out
I've never had a drink before.
Joy says, 'It's nothing special,
just your typical London pub.'
But for me, who doesn't know
what a typical London pub is,
it's like something out
of the Terry Pratchett book
I read on the plane here
or one of those old English movies
I watched with Mama.
It's a 'ramshackle old pub', Joy says,
large but still cosy, all mismatched armchairs
with floral and velvet upholstery.
The creaky wooden floors are painted black
and a variety of lights from fairy lights
to chandeliers attempt to brighten it up
and almost succeed.
The place isn't too busy either,
so Joy and I take the three
completely incompatible armchairs
by the fireplace, and as I sit down heavily,
feeling all my tiredness,
Joy goes to get us drinks.
I watch the flames flicker comfortingly
in the fireplace and feel sleep slowly lull me.

'It's Rum O'Clock!'

I jerk awake to the sound of Joy's voice
and open my eyes to what looks like an iced Coke before me.

She clinks the side of her glass with mine
and we both take a sip. She watches for my reaction

and chuckles as I screw up my face at the taste.
'It's only a single! Don't worry. You'll get used to it.'

I'm glad she's not offended, and honestly,
I'm glad my first drink is with Joy.

She has such a compassionate way about her.
'Thanks for the drink,' I say, remembering my manners.

She waves it away. 'You just get me one next time.'
Her generosity after my night of terror almost makes me cry.

Before I can tell her this, a girl comes out of nowhere
and jumps on Joy and hugs her tight.

Joy hugs her back and they laugh as the other girl
almost falls off Joy's lap.

'Paro, meet Alexia.'
Alexia comes and gives me a warm hug.

Alexia

Is the kind of exquisite that you see in paintings,
all lustrous curls and big brown eyes,

her dark skin reflecting gold from the flames in the fireplace.
She's dressed simply in a white shirt with rolled-up sleeves,

and a pair of jeans, an easy smile across her face.
She's quieter than Joy, likes to listen more than talk,

but everything she speaks of is so cerebral yet full of passion. She's
studying filmmaking and she tells me,

'I want to create work that invents
a space rather than fills up a space that was already there.'

And just that one sentence leaves me thoughtful for hours.
Her newest short film is about what the world would be like

if all humans developed the ability to truly hear each other
and let empathy guide society rather than money.

It sounds like magic to me.
I can see why Joy and she are friends.

They share kindness and warmth in two unique ways.
They call each other Goddesses and Queens,

Women who love other women this way are an ode
to sisterhood in a way I have not experienced yet.

Joy pulls me out of my reverie as she announces,
'Paro's from India and she's doing illustration with me!'

Joy turns to me. 'Show her your Tarot drawings.'
I start to whinge, 'Uh ... no, they're—'

Joy's brow furrows,
'Don't you start putting yourself down again.'

I pout theatrically and hand over my book to her.
Alexia flips through the pages and her eyes sparkle.

'These are great! I've never seen Tarot illustrations like this!
Who are the figures you're drawing?'

I beam, basking in the validation.
'They're the Gods and Goddesses from Hindu mythology.'

She looks through the book for a minute longer
then asks, 'Do you read Tarot?'

'Yes,' I say. 'All the women in my family do.'
Joy and Alexia look at each other and then back at me.

'Will you read ours?' It's almost in unison.
I pause. I've never read Tarot for anyone

but myself and my brother before.
What if I am terrible at reading for other people?

What if I make them anxious with my reading?
Or just don't read properly at all?

But they both look so excited as they wait for an answer,
I can't bear to tell them no.

So I take a long sip of my drink for courage and say,
'Yes. How about at my flat tomorrow?'

Accents

When I turn the key to the flat,
I can hear faint music playing inside.

I realise I don't even know my flatmates
because yesterday I just wanted to run and hide.

I follow the music to the kitchen.
There are three people in there,

they all seem friendly –
with each other at least.

I quietly move to the fridge to put away the milk I bought.
The girl at the stove notices me.

'Hi! I'm Jen.' She has bright blue eyes,
and is wearing a Cath Kidston flowery apron.

'Paro.'
I shake her hand.

'Oh, I love your accent,' she tells me.
'Where are you from?'

'India.' I say, although India is a huge country.
The people in Kashmir are different from the people

in Punjab, or Kerala or Bengal or Rajasthan.
Each state has a different food and language.

It's hard to explain all that though,
so I just say, 'India.'

'Oh, you're from India?'
says a boy with blond hair hanging in his eyes.

'That's so cool. I went to Delhi once.
Jonathan. Nice to meet you.'

'Nice to meet you too,' I relax and smile slightly.
'My parents live in Delhi. Where did you go?'

The pale girl in the corner of my eye,
with dyed jet-black hair and glasses

suddenly starts laughing and the other two stare at her.
'Sorry. It's just that you speak kind of funny.

You mix up your Vs and Ws.
"*Vhere did you go?*"' She laughs as she says it.

I freeze. Then take a deep breath to calm myself
and go back to stocking my food away.

When I turn back, she's pulling out her phone.
'Can you say, "Hello, how are you?"'

She says it like the *Simpsons*' character Apu.
No one I know sounds like that.

It looks like she's going to take a video of me,
and I don't know what comes over me,

but I look at her coldly and,
pronouncing each word slowly, I state,

'I am *not* your Indian performing monkey.'
She puts her phone down and rolls her eyes at me.

'Calm down.
It was just a joke. Jeez.'

I say nothing. I look at Jen and Jonathan,
but they have busied themselves with their cooking.

After a few tense minutes, I return to my room
and call campus security about last night.

The man tells me, 'Thanks for letting us know.
Sorry that happened to you,' but doesn't say anything more.

Later, I sit at my table with a brand new notebook.
I want to write to lessen all this burden I am carrying.

But the pen doesn't move.
No words come out.

And I realise, maybe when I deserted poetry,
it deserted me too.

If I Could Still Write Poetry I Would Write: Bilingual

I hold two different languages in my mouth.
One is my mother tongue, from earth and family.
The other is the colonisers', from war and blood.

Sometimes I think my mouth is too small for both.
I mix syllables up. Words don't feel like they fit right.
The longer I speak English, the further Hindi feels.

What is the English word for dil?
I used to ask my mother when I was little.
She would kiss my forehead and say, *heart.*

Now I feel like I constantly reach for words
in Hindi and only find them in English.
This too is a learning, how to get better at balancing both.

I have two words in my head for mother,
two words for God, two words for country,
two words for love.

All of these are blessings –
my emotions sing
a two-voiced song –

and it doesn't matter if I cannot pronounce
English words perfectly. I carry my roots on my tongue.
The way I speak is a testament to where I came from.

For that, I refuse to let anyone make me feel small.

Joy's Flat

I decide against bringing Alexia and Joy to my flat.
Something about yesterday didn't feel safe.
My flat went from a place of safety to just somewhere I stay.

So I take my cards, put them in my backpack,
and head towards Joy's flat where she lives with her parents.
I bump into Alexia at the foot of her building.

Alexia greets me with a huge hug. It truly feels
like we have known each other for ever
and not just met once.

'You're going to LOVE Joy's mum,'
she says as we walk up the stairs.
She doesn't ask why I changed our plans.

We knock on door number 70. Then wait and knock again.
We hear Joy shout, 'I'm here! I'mhereI'mhereI'mhere!'
She opens the door, in a pink hoodie covered in paint marks.

Alexia puts her hands on her hips.
'Always late! You knew we were coming!'
Joy laughs, hugs her. 'I forgot. I was painting.'

I pull a comically pained expression
press the back of my hand to my forehead.
'I'm so *hurt*!'

We all dissolve into giggles when a voice calls out,
'Are you all going to keep cackling like witches
or come inside and say hello?'

'Yes, Mum!' Joy rolls her eyes and ushers us in,
and we follow her through the cheery yellow corridor
full of family pictures to the kitchen,

where the delicious scent of spices is coming from.
A tall, slender woman in a blue and white floral dress
turns to us. She looks like a slightly older version of Joy,

same dark skin, same gentle smile, same beautiful dimples.
She embraces Alexia, then looks at me. 'You must be Paro.'
I nod and hug her as she says, 'Joy has told me all about you.'

'Only bad things,' Joy promises me
and then howls theatrically as her mother pinches her ear.
'Don't listen to this one – she just loves being cheeky.'

The Truth About Mothers Who Love Their Daughters

Is that you can sense it from the minute
you meet them, the way they carry us
even when we are grown.

The way they teach us the world may not be fair
but it is still ours to mould
and shape and make our own.

They change themselves
to learn best to accept us,
still nurture us when they disagree.

Their love evolves and grows us,
and they don't want us to be a reflection of themselves,
but who we truly are, and who we are meant to be.

That's the feeling I got,
when I saw Joy
with her mother today.

The Reading

Joy's room is perfect for a reading.
Her walls are pale blue and covered
in her beautiful illustrations.

Joy's work is all about celebrating
black womanhood, and her passion project
is painting black women from all across London.

On the easel she currently has in her room
is an intricate blue and pink portrait
of a seven-year-old girl who is her neighbour.

I stare at it transfixed for a few moments,
lost in the colours, until Joy asks, 'Ready to read?'
and I leave my dreamlike trance and nod.

She lights a white candle at my request,
and the three of us sit on her bed,
holding hands and saying a prayer

for protection and guidance
from the universe.
I shuffle the cards

and start with Alexia. Do the ritual.
Then I tell her to ask a question.
She asks about her love life.
I fan out the cards before her
and make her choose three.
She chooses:

The Ace of Wands: past position.
'Someone has recently entered your life.
A passionate new beginning.'

The Five of Cups: present position.
'Either one or both of you are full of
regret and not paying attention to what's before you.'

The Knight of Cups: future position.
'An offer of love is coming your way soon.
The knight brings a chalice with him.'

Alexia looks at me in surprise.
'You can see that in the cards?'
I put the cards back in the deck nervously. 'Were they right?'

'I've been fighting with my girlfriend,'
she says after a short pause, 'about something
that now seems silly. Can I ask more questions?'

My nerves disappear. So I wasn't bad at doing this for others.
I could really help. 'Of course. Just remember,
the cards show you one of infinite possibilities.'

Joy speaks from where
she is leaning against her headboard,
'What does that mean?'

'The Tarot is about showing you paths,
and your decisions lead you to infinite paths.
They give you clarity on problems, not 100 per cent accuracy.'

Alexia and Joy look at each other.
'Can you show us how to read them?'
I grin widely. 'Of course! But first, Joy, let's do yours.'

Joy's Pain

Joy seems uncharacteristically anxious.
I see it on her face. No big smile, no dimples or ease.
When she sits cross-legged before me,

she seems subdued.
'Are you sure you want to do this?'
I ask her gently, worried.

She nods. 'I just want to know,
will he come back into my life again.'
From behind her, Alexia frowns.

I don't ask her who.
The cards would tell all anyway.
I shuffle the cards,

quietly murmuring Joy's question.
Then I make her hold the pack
and go through the ritual I did with Alexia.

I say an extra special prayer
because Joy's face is so tense.
Fanning the cards out before her, I ask her to pick.

The Devil: past position.
'The person you are asking about was cruel
and there was a toxicity here.'

Six of Cups: present position.
'Beware of nostalgia which will lead you back
down that path towards him.'

Ace of Cups: future position.
'If you stay your course, a new love
and deep new connections are coming your way.'

I look at Joy and see tears in her eyes.
They slide down her face and she looks so vulnerable
I take her hands and ask tenderly, 'Who hurt you, Joy?'

And she tells me, as Alexia wraps her arm around her.
'He was my first boyfriend. He cheated on me and lied
so many times and I just never knew. He still calls.'

Her tears become sobs,
and Alexia and I both hug her hard
and just let her cry.

'It's my own fault. I should have known better.'

She sighs as the sobs subside.
I look at her in shock, 'Absolutely not, Joy.
You did nothing wrong. *He* hurt *you*.

Put the blame where it belongs.'
Alexia nods. 'Paro's right. This isn't your fault.'
We are all quiet for a few minutes

until Alexia says,
'Should Paro and I go smash his car windows?'

Joy cracks a smile.
'No don't do that.'

'Okay, how about we deflate all his tyres?'
I offer and Joy giggles a bit. 'No.'

'Okay, we'll be reasonable and just destroy his PlayStation,'
I declare and Alexia nods vigorously.

By the time we are done expanding
on the many ways we could prank Joy's ex,
the room is a blur of laughter for us all.

Calling Mama

On the way to the flat,
I can't stop thinking about Mama.

I know we haven't been close lately,
but suddenly I miss her.

Seeing Joy with her mother
made me miss my own terribly.

Our relationship may not be perfect,
but once upon a time

she told me stories.
She made me the person who I am.

When I get back,
I grab my phone from my bag.

It's still only 10 o'clock back home.
She's probably sitting with Papa

watching a TV show she likes after dinner.
I close my eyes, and imagine my parents

and my home, my brother making silly remarks
about what they are watching.

My mother throwing cushions at him
and my father belly-laughing at them both.

My hand presses *contacts*,
finds her number.

I press *call*.
'Beti Rani?' Her voice fills my head

as I clutch the phone close to my ear.
She hasn't called me that since I was little.

'Hi, Mama. Are you okay?'
I can hear the TV in the background,

the distant murmur of my brother
and father talking.

'We are fine. Indra is being silly.
We are watching that new Shah Rukh Khan movie.

Damini came to visit with her mother today.
She speaks fluent English now

and their business is doing so well.
They have their own house.

She said she missed you.
Indra sulked and said you were her favourite.'

I laugh,
but it sounds more like a sob,

'Are you okay, baby?' she asks,
her voice concerned now.

I'm not. I wish I could tell you,
but I don't want to worry you.

I'm sorry I didn't spend more time with you.
I can't wait to hug you again.

'Everything is fine, Mama.'
Then I add, 'I just called to say I miss you.'

She is quiet. For a second I think
she may have hung up.

But then she speaks,
her voice full of emotion.

'I miss you too.'

The First Month

I read somewhere the first month
of going away to university is the hardest.

After that you get busy.
They don't say it gets easier.

Just that you get busy – working, living, studying.
I'm lucky. I have friends who make me happy.

I see Devon around campus
and we stop and chat every now and then.

I am too shy to make a first move.
Besides, he always has another girl with him.

Instead, I focus on my art
and my newfound friends.

Joy and Alexia and I share the same brown eyes
and a ready laugh at each other's jokes.

and I thank the universe every day for them.
We are inseparable. We watch movies.

We cook for each other. We make art together.
Joy and I are both in Alexia's new film,

and Alexia posed for our illustrations in the studio.
We speak of our families and of love.

I tell them about Mahi. About how love
feels like it has deserted me since the day

my parents found out I was bi.
How I was once close to my mother,

but now it feels like we barely know each other.
Alexia tells me how hard it was

to come out as lesbian to her religious father.
He still refuses to speak to her.

I think about this a lot.
At least Mama still talks to me.

Alexia is so hopeful that things will
change with him, even though some days

she feels like she is forgetting him
and they were always so close.

It's strange how much our parents mould us,
even in the trauma of their absence.

Joy talks about how her grandfather passed away
when she was so little,

and she feels like her father and she
are still grieving him. He had brought them together.

We talk about England. Barbados. Nigeria. Kashmir.
As we explore London, we make art out of living memory.

I finally tell them what happened
at the flat and on the dark street.

'I was just shocked
that no one really does anything.'

Joy is heavy in thought as she walks beside me.
'Don't let it eat you up, babe. It'll kill you.'

I stop walking and stare at her.
'So you're saying I should get used to it?'

Joy stops too and shakes her head. 'Never.
I would never say that, you know that.

I'm saying turn it into art. I'm saying,
do what I do. Use your work to tell people, Paro.

Change the world with it.'

Alexia reaches out and squeezes my hand.
'Don't ever, ever get used to it.

Let it be fuel instead.'

Sam Calls

Just before the end of the month.
He's in Washington DC,
studying pre-med at Georgetown.

So when he calls me at 3 a.m.
on a Tuesday night and wakes me up
I am not too pleased.

'Sammm … it's three in the morning,'
I complain, eyes too heavy to open fully.

'Paro. Listen. I did it.'
His voice is nervous but excited.

'Did what?'
I ask, opening one eye slightly.

'I left Georgetown,'
he says loudly over the hum of people behind him.

'What?!'
I sit up now, suddenly wide awake.

'Listen, I had to. I don't want to be a doctor.'
Behind him an announcement nearly drowns him out.

'Where are you? Are you okay?'
I'm worried now, trying to think what I can do.

'Yeah! I'm going to art school!'
He laughs, elation steeped in his words.

'Sam! That's amazing!'
I squeal, and there is a thump on my wall.

I wince and lower my voice.
'Which school?'

'RISD. I'm going to study painting!'
His delight is at fever pitch and I can't help but smile.

'I'm so happy for you. You deserve the world,'
I say warmly, and I hug my knees close.

'I haven't told Mom yet,'
he says worriedly.

'She loves you, she'll get over it when you're famous,'
I tell him earnestly, and hear him laugh.

'I hope so.'
He sounds anxious but happy.

'Are you at the airport?'
I ask him.

'Yeah, and now I got to go catch my flight!'
I can hear Sam rummaging around his bags.

'Hey, Sam?'
I say, gently.

'Just so you know,
I'm really proud of you.'

'Thanks, Paro. I knew you'd be.'
And I can hear his grin through the phone.

Instead of Sunday Roast

There is a quiet legacy
I practise as ritual on Sundays now.

When people here put together
their Sunday roasts,

I get up early
to marinate the meat for Rogan Josh.

Bring out the milk and rice
and almonds for sweet phirni.

I pull out the spices
and line them up carefully by the hob,

and as I count them –
coriander, cloves, bay leaves, cardamom, cinnamon –

I remember the stories my nani told me.
And suddenly I am eleven years old again,

standing in my nani's kitchen
fragranced with these same spices,

learning about love, loss and my family history
steeped in heroism and strength through these recipes.

We may have lost everything in partition.
But at least we kept the roots in recipes.

The Visit

Maybe it is because
I am more melancholy on Sundays

or maybe it is the fact that
I made phirni with badam pista

to remember Nani,
but that night at two in the morning,

when the moonlight comes in quietly,
gently through the blinds,

I see Ganesh appear in my small room.
The forever jovial, four-armed

elephant God. He isn't in his full form,
more a small statue come to life on my bedside.

This visit is different.
A part of me feels like I already know him.

The others were an enigmatic mystery,
but with him, there is a familiarity.

I already know what he will say
long before he says it.

'Let me tell you a story.'

The Seventh Story

There is security in nothingness. The celestial womb I floated in for thousands of years doing nothing but being energy. We all float through the cosmos, lacking self-awareness before birth comes and takes us. My birth was unusual, even by celestial standards. I was not born with an elephant head. This came later. My father had gone for penance, and penance then lasted years. My mother, a Goddess, crafted the form of a boy from turmeric paste. When she completed her masterpiece, she breathed life into it.

This is where I came from. For years, I was my mother's sole protector as she had asked me to be. When she slept, I watched over her. When she went to bathe in the holy mountain, I guarded her so no one could see her. I knew no man or woman, no being other than her. So years later when my father returned, blue-skinned, snake around his neck, a river falling from his hair, I did not know him. Did not know my own father was the Great Destroyer God Shiva. The tragedy was, he, too, did not know me. When I saw him approaching, I stood fast in my position, guarding my mother from being seen while bathing.

'Let me pass, child. I wish to see my wife.'

I did not move. 'I cannot. My mother has told me no one may enter.'

My father was not known for his sweet temper. His impatience and fury at being blocked from his own home by a strange young boy soon got the better of him. In a fit of rage, he lifted his trident, severed my head, and entered the mountain. There, they were united and it was not until later that my mother came out to find my body on the ground. Her devastation, it is said, could be heard across the world. She revealed my identity to my father and told him he had just committed the ultimate celestial imbalance by killing his own son. Upon learning who I was, my father was filled with regret and sorrow. His grief was further multiplied when he learned of my unconditional love for my mother, that I would, even as a child, have given my life to protect her honour.

Few know this about my father, but although he is quick in his fury, he is also quick to please. Instantly, he lifted his wife into his arms and promised her he would bring her son back to her. He called his bull Nandi and told him to bring back the head of the first animal who would give it. Nandi found an elephant calf and prayed to it, asking for its head in return for becoming an eternal life in Devlok. The calf gave up its head and its mortal life, and Nandi returned with it.

And so, my father placed the elephant calf's head on my body and brought me back to life. And although my mother's heart was full of joy and she embraced me, and I rejoiced in her love, something still troubled her heart. My father knew my mother well, he knew what had crept into her mind and sunk its claws into her thoughts. She worried who would accept an elephant-headed God. So my father called together all of the Gods and asked them to bless me. He recognised me as his own son and gave me my name, Ganesh, Ganpati. I was given the blessing of being worshipped first, before any other Goddess or God.

My mother's love brought me to life not once but twice, and made me the God I am.

After the Seventh Story

Paro: Have we met before?

Ganesh: We have all met before. That is how reincarnation works.

Paro: No, I mean … never mind. Are you telling me that I must make amends with my mother?

Ganesh: There are no amends to make if a relationship is still there. You need to rebuild what was there before. It is up to you. Your dharma.

Paro: Perhaps it is easier for you to say, given who your mother is.

Ganesh: But my relationship with my father only started after my death. And through generosity and forgiveness, our bond only grew stronger.

Paro: Do you ever feel resentment? Do you ever miss the human head you once had?

Ganesh: No. Never. For if I did not have this head, I would never have been able to create one of my greatest treasures.

Paro: What was that?

Ganesh: I broke off my own tusk and used it to write the Mahabharata.

I Think I May Understand

Why they are still visiting me.
But the truth is hidden in the corner of my eye
just out of sight.

Every time I think I have caught it,
it slips away from me like the twilight
slips from the day's grasp.

Years ago, my mother gave me a ring
with Ganesh carved into it.
I carried it with me everywhere.

But today is the first time I wear it.

Discoveries

I started doing
day-long illustration marathons
to deliberately lose track of time
when I was fifteen.

Letting my work consume me
was the only way to get over Mahi.
It worked as well as it could.
The pain dulled as I thought of her less.

I should have known that
what we bury
will always return
to haunt us.

Today, I am creating Saraswati,
the Goddess of wisdom and intellect
as the High Priestess.
As I add stars to the background,

my phone *dings*
and I nearly jump out of my skin.
Sighing, I reach for it
and my eyes focus on the screen.

It's a friend request.
From *Mahi*.

My hand drops my paintbrush,
leaving an ugly dollop of white paint
across my pristine painting,
but in that moment I barely notice it.

My stomach clenches
as I stare at it.
Finally, heart beating fast,
I look at her account.

She's in Mumbai now.
Studying biochemistry.
I look at her friend list
and don't see Priya or Shalini.

And she still looks exactly like
the Goddess Girl that I remember her to be.
Her profile picture is her
sitting on the sand

of a sunny beach, drink in hand.
She's looking sideways at the camera,
eyes still pearl-like and glowing
… and full of secrets.

I'm about to put the phone down
to take deep breaths and steady myself
when something catches my eye.
Her hand that holds the drink …

… I open up the picture and zoom closer,
then squint to see clearer.
There, pixellated on her thumb,
I can make out the ring.

The ring I gave her at Dilli Haat.
She kept it all this time.
My heart aches as I realise
I was not the only one grieving and full of regret.

My finger hovers the friend request
And I press

Accept

The Review (or the Day That's Been Giving Me Nightmares for Months)

There are few words that can fully describe
the dread that shifts in your stomach
when you do your first ever review.

A bad grade will break Papa's heart more than mine.
A bad grade could lead to me failing out of the class.
A bad grade could —

'Paro Mad-error?'

Why can they never pronounce my last name?
I grumble as I carry my portfolio into the classroom.
The head of department and my teacher,

they're both wearing sombre shades
of grey and black clothing.
I try not to think of Yama,

the God of Death, hovering over the ashes
of my creative dreams and hopes,
the buffalo he rides roaring furiously at me.

My teacher, Jane, is older,
and looks so Picture-Perfect Professional in suits
that one almost forgets she's an art teacher.

Sharon, the HoD, is usually in bright pinks,
peacock blues, a strange hairclip in her short blonde hair.
She's always shiny and happy; it's strange to see her this way.

'Show us where you are at with your project on ...'
Jane squints at the list.
'Mythology-inspired Tarot cards.'

It's not a good sign that she can't remember
what I'm doing off the top of her head.
It means my pitch hasn't made an impression.

Trying not to panic, I carefully pull out my work.
They study it, and my body feels as wobbly
        as a badly made raft in a lake.

One push
And I could

                        S

                    I

                        N

                            K

After a few agonising minutes
that feel like hours,
Jane says,

'These are good.
            But good does not a great artist make.'

D

'I can't believe it.'
Alexia slides into the booth next to me,
throwing her bag in the corner.
'How could they give you a D?'

Joy has gone to get us drinks
while we sit at the corner table in a pub.
I am brooding. I move from
intense despair to fury and then to self-hatred;

and all of it happens in the span of seconds.
It feels like someone has stolen my purpose for living.
'Apparently, I'm good, but not great,'
I say bitterly as I lay my forehead on the table.

Joy is back now, drinks in hand.
'Do you know how many
great artists were told they weren't great?'
I take a sip of my drink and glumly reply,

'But lots of good artists didn't
become great either.'
They trade a look, and Alexia's eyes
are gentle when they turn back to me.

'It's only first year –
you can prove them wrong.'
I dip my head sadly
but don't say anything.

'I know what'll cheer you up!'
Joy slams her hands
on the table.
'Let's go out out!'

Out Out

It took me some time to understand what this means,
but Jonathan, my flatmate, explained it to me.

'It's when you go out for the evening
but make sure you don't have plans the next day

because you're going to stay out late
and party *hard*.'

So I think I know what to expect
when we all go home to change.

I've just about finished putting my jeans on
when I hear a knock at the door.

Joy and Alexia are here.
I open the door and let them in.

'We didn't even plan this,'
Joy remarks as we look at each other.

We are all wearing black jeans
and high-heeled boots.

Joy is wearing a white sleeveless vest.
I'm in a black ribbed top.

Alexia has on a pinstriped waistcoat and laughs.
'Beth is going to say we look like a girl band.'

Beth is Alexia's girlfriend. She's a sculptor,
and they have a turbulent relationship.

They're always either fighting
or declaring intense love for each other.

One thing is for sure, tonight won't be a boring night out,
I think as we make our way to Soho.

The streets of London are otherworldly at night,
as though it is a Wonderland that turned from forest

to concrete. Bright neon lights, the distant soundtrack
of sirens and people laugh-screaming.

When we reach Soho, I almost laugh,
because the name of the first club we go to is

The Rabbit Hole.

The Incident

Don't be prey.
The words ring in my ears,
throbbing louder than the music.

It takes me by surprise.
I don't know why I'm thinking of it.
Alexia disappears to find Beth.

Don't be prey.
Papa's words won't leave me alone.
Joy notices my face. 'Are you okay?'

I nod and yell, 'It's just loud!'
I feel bad about lying to her,
but I would feel worse if I left them suddenly.

Instead I look around the club.
The dance floor is packed full of people,
a sixties disco ball circles from the ceiling.

People are standing in corners,
kissing and doing a whole lot more.
I avert my eyes and look elsewhere.

The bar is lit up by blue lights
and people pack around it,
pushing each other

to get the bartender's attention.
Someone grabs my arm and I whip around –
it's just Alexia. She hands me a drink.

'Thanks!' I take it from her.
'Next one is on me!'
Joy is being chatted up by a guy in a suit.

I give Beth a hug.
She's dyed her hair blue at the ends,
and she looks like a mermaid.

I tell her so and she laughs.
'Al said the same thing.'
I like how she has a nickname for her.

Something special to make Alexia her own.
I wonder if one day someone will give me
a nickname too.

I buy the next round for everyone,
even Joy's new friend –
only because he makes her smile.

We dance to Avicii,
and for a while I forget everything,
other than the music as it takes over me.

Eventually I need to stop.
'I'll just be back!' I yell to Alexia who nods,
gesturing to the sign for the loo.

Squeezing my way through the sweaty bodies
across the dance floor,
I feel like a mess of other people's odours

and perfumes by the time I get there.
But then I find a big arm blocking my way.
'Hi,' the owner of the arm says to me.

'Hi,' I speak loudly. 'Can I get past, please?'
He's clearly older, easily in his thirties,
a close-cropped haircut and a button-down shirt.

'Not until you give me your number.'
I roll my eyes, I can smell alcohol on his breath.
'I'm eighteen.'

He leers at me, slightly swaying.
'That's cool. I like them young.'
I grimace in disgust, push past him, and –

feel a hand grab a fistful of my hair
and yank me back against a sweaty body.
I freeze as his mouth whispers in my ear,

'Cocky bitch!'
He shoves my face into the wall.
'Now be a good girl.'

I feel his large sweaty hand pawing at my top
and another fiddling with the buttons on my jeans.
This can't be happening!

It's a busy nightclub,
how can no one see what he is doing?
But the music is so loud,

so many people here dancing, partying,
you KNOW how easy it is to get lost in a crowd.
I open my mouth but I can't make a sound.

I am seven again, at the bazaar, not knowing
what is going to happen to me.
His hand is inside my jeans,

and I hear a voice in my head say,
'Do something! You aren't seven any more!'
I start to struggle hard against him,

a scream rises in my throat,
but he clamps his free hand over my mouth.
My mind races until I remember I have on heels.

I raise my leg as high as I can
and bring my heel down HARD on his foot.
He screams and falls backwards.

I should run, but instead
I launch myself at him
and we both tumble to the ground.

I am kicking and screaming
and biting and clawing
and yelling at him:

'HOW DARE YOU!
HOW DARE YOU!
HOW DARE YOU!'

He shrieks in a way
I've never heard
a human shriek before.

Strong hands pull me off him,
pulling me back forcefully by my waist,
and by the time the red mist fades

I see the damage I have done.
I see the man moaning on the floor,
I see people staring at me like I am crazy.

The music has stopped.
A bouncer appears to escort me through the crowd.
'Get out of here!' He pushes me out onto the street.

'But he assaulted me first!'
I can already feel a bruise growing on my face
from where it made contact with the wall.

But it's too late.
The bouncer is already gone and I am alone.
I take out my phone to text my friends,

but find I am shaking too hard to type.
My head still ringing,
I give up and sit on the pavement.

A part of me is proud for defending myself.
The other is terrified of what I am capable of.
How long has this been hiding in me?

Don't be prey,
my father had told me.
Am I the predator now?

The Darkness

It's strange how the streets can turn
from candyfloss and pastel-blue neon lights,
full of drunk people enjoying their night,
to danger lurking on every corner,
every sound violent, a snake's mouth
snapping shut suddenly making you jump.

I feel like my skin is on too tight.
I find it difficult to breathe.
The phone screen lights up.
It's Alexia. 'Paro, where are you?'
Another text from Joy.
'Call us pls.'

My hands are still shaking too much.
I look up at the sky for a minute,
hoping there is an answer there,
but I find none.
Nothing glimmers
to tell me right from wrong.

We do not come because you want us to,
Shikhandi had said.
I swallow down bile as it rises in my throat,
take a deep breath, and get unsteadily to my feet.
A whiff of sulphur catches me off guard.
And then I see her, standing under a streetlight.

Blue-skinned goddess,
hair wild in the light September breeze.
Eyes so wide you can see the whites
even from this distance,
red tongue out, fangs for all to see.
It *is* her. Kali.

Kali

People walk past her like she isn't there at all,
but she's standing there so clear for me to see.
Skulls around her neck, eyes fixed on me.
I walk over to her until I can hear her, feel the sulphur rise.

'You are older now.' Her voice reverberates.
It is the same one I heard in my head before
I lunged at the man in the nightclub.
'Old enough to hear this story.'

The Eighth Story

There is only one Goddess who is named carnage. One Goddess who is distilled anger in woman form and who causes such fear that they have misplaced her story of origin.

There are three versions.

In one tale, I was born terrifying. On the battlefields where Gods fought demons, and no one wanted to make the demons bleed because what good are Gods without their piety? So, instead, I was conjured from the Goddess Durga's head, bloodthirsty and angry.

In the second, I was born from ashes. When Shiva tricked the Mahadevi, Mother Goddess to us all, and made her give him her powers, from her ashes, I was born. Women do this – we are able to resurrect ourselves from the ashes of what others do to us.

In the third, I was born to be every mother's uncontrollable rage from the womb of the Goddess of Love. A riot in a woman's body when she found her beheaded son Ganesh. I waged war on this earth, poured destruction into everything that existed here. I was the vengeance the Gods could not silence, no matter how hard they tried. They had to beg and plead that I control my anger and put it aside.

All three are true. All three are not true. It doesn't matter. People lie all the time to each other. Lies become rumours, rumours become legends, legends turn into myth, and Gods and Goddesses are born. It's why we reincarnate so often. To tell another story.

What does not change is our purpose. I was born to drain the wicked from the earth. They cannot change this about me.

So let me tell you the real story.

While the Lord Vishnu lay asleep, two demons who presumed the world was unprotected attacked Brahma and the world he had just created. Their names were Madhu and Kaitabha. They were malevolent forces born to destroy the world, love, the universe itself. They wanted to lay waste to everything. My sister, the Goddess Yoga Nidra, ran to Vishnu's sleeping form in terror and pleaded with him to wake up so as to kill the demons.

But the God was in a deep sleep, and from his dreams I was born. In his absence, I waged war against Madhu and Kaitabha. I used anger as a weapon, I used chaos as valour, I even became the illusion they desired to tame them into submission. When I was close enough to bring them to their knees, Vishnu appeared and slaughtered them. They will tell you I am not beautiful. I agree. I was never meant to be.

I am chaos. I am the rage they quiver before. I carry within me an anger so powerful that even the Gods are afraid of me. Even in power they want us to be pretty. They expect us to be palatable, easy to digest, as though we are some small meal but, dear one, I am proof we do not have to be. We can be a war cry and a violence. We can be as ugly as we want to be. Hard to swallow. Unsettling to look at. A fire in the bones. A macabre they fear.

What happened to you is the first of many tragedies too many women go through, but this does not have to define you.

You too can be like me. I am a Goddess of duality. Sometimes I sit on a throne of corpses, and sometimes the Gods themselves hold up my throne. I challenge their sense of what is womanly, wear my hair untamed – the Goddess of darkness but also righteous fury. Whatever I am, they find it hard to accept me. I am a dialogue between what is carnal and what is glory. Let yourself be like me, and become an enigma too. But here is the trick, dear one. Learn it well. Wear your hair wild, embrace your anger and learn to wield it without fear as a sword against those who hurt you.

The Walk Back

I text my friends,
'Sorry. Something bad happened.
I'm okay but I need to be alone.
I promise I'll explain when I see you again.
I'm sorry for being a bad friend.'

Then I start walking.
Kali didn't stay to talk,
but I didn't expect her to.
I catch the Central and then the Northern Line
and step out into the lonely street.

I should be afraid.
This street holds fear for me.
But tonight fear has taken a back seat.
I walk with purpose to the flat
and go straight to my room.

Then I sit at my table,
place the blank notebook
in front of me,
start writing,

and do not stop until dawn.

For Girls Made of Fire

(A Page From Paro's Notebook)

Girl,
you were born with a fire inside you,
and this world is determined to stamp it out.

You will see it when you stand up for yourself
and you are told, *'It isn't ladylike to raise your voice.'*

You will hear it when you wear something that hugs your body
and feel the uncomfortable sensation of being stripped naked
by the eyes of men who call you names you are still too young to
understand.

You will know it when a man tries to use his strength
to have his way with you the first time,
and you need to use your fists/teeth/legs to get him off.

You will understand it when you see
your mother's eyes filled with terror
because you are an hour later than you said you would be.

But you must never let them take
those flames down from within your soul.
Instead, you must burn brighter than ever
because you are a Daughter of the Divine
and you belong only to yourself, *not to this world.*

Dawn

The sun rose quietly, leaving striped rays
on my desk. I laid my pen down finally
and looked out of the window
as the cold mist blew around the city,
the roofs of buildings shadows
against a soft orange-gold sky.

For a moment, I am still,
and no thoughts disturb my peace.
Nothing haunts me in the silence.
A calm has washed over me.

'Is this what it feels like
when the poetry comes back to you?'

I ask the empty room quietly.
The sun rays glint against
the Ganesh carving
on my ring.

I feel like I can hear his voice say,
'Yes.'
This is what it feels like.
This is what it feels like.

An Apology

When I get out of the shower,
I open my bedroom door to find
two Goddesses standing in my room.
Except these aren't the apparitions
I've been seeing.

Alexia and Joy stare at me, full of questions.
'Paro, why did you just disappear last night?'
Joy asks, clearly upset. 'We were so scared!'
'We thought something had happened
to you,' Alexia adds, worry in her eyes.

They stop when they see my face clearly.
The bruise has swollen, an ugly purple,
red and blue across my cheekbone.
'Oh my days, what happened?!'
Joy looks like she is going to cry.

'Is this why you left?' Alexia is furious.
'Have you been to the doctor?
Who did this to you?!'
I try to lighten the mood by pointing at my face.
'Oh, this? You should see the other guy.'

Neither of them laugh.
They simply look at me,
eyes filled with so much concern.
I sigh and sit down heavily
on the edge of my bed.

'I'm really sorry I worried you.
There was this man and …'
I swallow hard. 'And he …
Let's just say he brought back
hurtful memories.'

Slowly, I unravel my deepest secret.
The fruit seller. The bazaar.
The man at the nightclub.
The assault. My frenzy.
The aftermath.

When I am done,
I look up at them.
'I'm sorry,' I repeat.
Joy wraps an arm around me.
'Don't apologise, babe.'

'None of it was your fault,'
Alexia firmly declares
as she grabs
both Joy and me
in a protective bear hug.

Sometimes all it takes
to help someone survive
anything brutal
are those six words:
'None of it was your fault.'

Find sisters, Ratri had said.

I finally understood
what she meant.

What I Have Learned About Sisterhood

Fill your life with women who empower you,
who help you believe in your magic,
and help them to believe in their own
exceptional power and incredible magic too.

Women who believe in each other can survive anything.
Women who believe in each other create armies
that will win kingdoms and wars.

Remember always,
the only people who can save us are each other,
the only people who can love us are ourselves.

The Diwali Party

Home is calling my name
louder today than it ever has.

I hear it in the tightness of Mama's voice.
I hear it in the way Nani says, 'I love you.'

I even hear it in Papa's voice,
and I think Indra is just annoyed I'm not there.

I wish I could explain to them I miss them too.
Guilt is becoming my best friend here.

I would spend Diwali alone reading,
trying to distract myself.

As I reach for poet Amrita Pritam's collected works
an invitation falls out and to the floor.

It's the one Sakshi gave me at the Desi Community,
and suddenly I know exactly how I will spend Diwali.

*

Sakshi's house is a large, red-sloped-roof house,
which makes the flat look like a tiny studio.

Three storeys high and each window
has a little LED candle.

You can see it from a distance;
it glows with warmth and chatter

while the other houses are quiet.
I bring a bottle of wine with me.

My mother always says
never to go to someone's house empty-handed.

I knock on the door,
and Sakshi opens it.

'You made it! Yay!'
Her smile is infectious.

'Happy Diwali!' I hand her the wine
and give her a big hug.

'Thank you! Happy Diwali!
Come inside, come inside!'

Mama would love Sakshi.
She's the sociable, warm, friendly girl

my mother wished I was,
but never, ever could be.

As soon as I think this, I hear Joy yelling in my head
about comparison and stop instantly.

I follow her into the massive living room.
The fragrance of sugary ladoos and samosas

follows me everywhere.
And there, in a room full of at least thirty people,

I see him. In a blue kurta and jeans,
engrossed in conversation. It's Devon.

I'd be lying to myself if I pretend
there isn't something there I want to explore.

Devon has those deep, inquisitive eyes,
a soft way about him.

I've seen the way he always has time for everyone
and doesn't play the popularity game at all.

Still, he makes me nervous
in the way Mahi used to make me nervous.

Yet he seems so familiar.
Like we've met somewhere before.

He catches my eye and excuses himself
to saunter over. 'Hey!' he says.

Sakshi looks between us. 'Do you two know each other?'
Devon nods. 'Yeah, we've met. Paro, you look lovely.'

I blush and instantly rebuke myself for blushing. 'Hi.'
'Good, let me get you a drink! Wine?' asks Sakshi.

'Yes, please! White if you have it,' I answer cheerfully.
'Of course!' She nods and disappears into the crowd.

I look back at Devon,
and suddenly there is no one else in the room but him.

His Smile Makes Me Feel Weak at the Knees

'Happy Diwali!'
I say, suddenly embarrassed I am staring.

'To you too,'
he wishes me back.

'How have you been?'
we both ask each other at once.

We laugh,
then he clears his throat.

'Paro, I've wanted to ask you
something for a while now.'

I tilt my head and look at him.
Was he going to do what I think?

He raises his hand to scratch his head
and I notice the tattoo on his forearm.

Lord Shiva's trishul. Before I can mention it,
he has put his arm down.

'Do you think you'd like to have dinner sometime?
Just you and me?'

There are butterflies in my stomach
and I feel like I am floating.

Is this how easy it is to just ask someone out?
I wish I had tried this with Mahi.

'I ...' I take a deep, deep breath
before speaking again.

'I like you, Devon,
I would like to see where this goes,

but you should know
I'm bisexual. I've loved a girl before.

If you're okay with that,
I'd love to go on a date with you.'

It's the first time I've said it out loud.
And a deep relief and pride floods through me.

He seems surprised, but his face clears quickly
into appreciation. 'Thanks for being honest.'

I don't say,
Thanks, I never used to be.

It feels like a big step for me.
I wait for his answer, trying to look composed.

'It doesn't change a thing.
I like you, Paro. A lot.'

I let go of the breath I didn't know I was holding.
'Oh, that's good.' Not knowing what else to say.

'Have other guys backed out because you're bisexual?'
He is incredulous and then angry, 'That's horrendously bigoted!'

'No!' I say quickly.
'I haven't … really dated guys before.'

I think about mentioning Mahi,
but then slowly shut that door.

A puzzled look comes over his face.
He is about to ask a question,

but just then Sakshi shows up with my wine
and scolds Devon. 'Stop monopolising her!

I want her to meet everyone.'

326

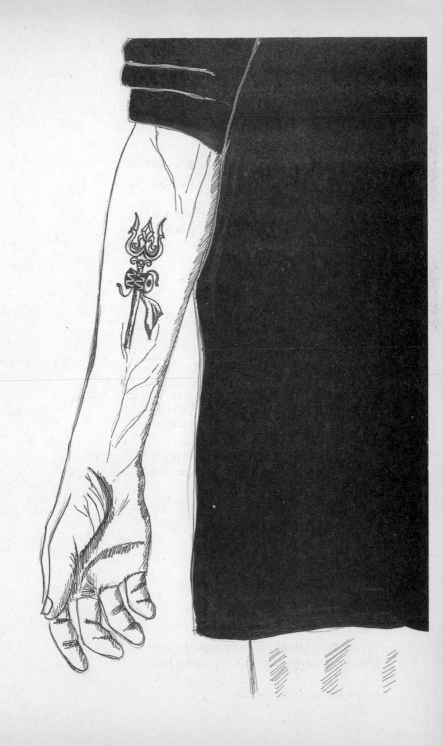

The Phone Call

Sakshi asks me to stay longer,
and I want to stay,
but there is something I need to do.

I say my goodbyes
and travel back,
heart thudding the entire way.

This may be the bravest thing I do.
I sit on my bed cross-legged,
pick up my phone and call.

'Hello?' Mama says.
My chest tightens.
I may burst.

'Hi, Mama. Please just listen, okay?'
Taking the silence as confirmation,
I say,

'Mama, I know you're not comfortable
talking about this. And we have never spoken of it.
But it's important to me you acknowledge this:

I'm bisexual. I don't just like boys.
And for a very long time, I thought that was wrong.
That I was dirty because of it somehow.

And now I know I am not.
I am not wrong for who I love
because love is a beautiful thing.

You're the one who taught me that,
with all your kindness and generosity.
So all I wanted to do, was call and tell you

I'm still your daughter, Mama, and I love you.
But I will not change this about myself.
It's who I will always be.'

I sit back and close my eyes,
waiting for my mother to tell me off,
or worse, just hang up.

Instead, I hear:
'Paro, I've had a long time to think about this.
I'm sorry I sent you away then.

I didn't know how to handle it at the time.
But now I know better.
I've been reading books

and trying to understand
since you left. It doesn't matter to me
who you love as long as they love you back.

You're my daughter, Paro.
And I will love you always, no matter what.
Never ever doubt that.'

I feel the tears running down my face
only after she stops speaking.
I pull my legs to my chest and cry in earnest.

I feel a thousand times lighter suddenly.
'Love you, Mama.'
'Love you too, Beti Rani.'

I can hear her voice heavy with emotion,
heavy with tears we can cry together now.
After a few minutes of quiet, I hear her say,

'When you come back,
let's go visit the Goddess
at Vaishno Devi.'

The Book

I find it in my room after class.
I'm used to waking up to Goddesses,
so the book does not surprise me.

In fact,
everything has been making sense lately,
and I feel oddly at peace.

Tomorrow I am spending the day
helping Joy move across the city
into an apartment with Alexia.

Later today, I am supposed to meet Devon,
we are going to paint together,
like we did on our first date months ago.

Today is also the day I got my final grade.
It isn't an A. It's a B.
But I don't mind.

I understand now
that progress,
true progress, is slow.

One foot after the other
teaches you more
than long, giant leaps.

Life finally feels like it is coming together
in the way of small miracles
and found families and inner peace.

So I know from the moment I see it
on my desk by the open window,
that this has been left for me.

They know me so well,
for what else would a poet cherish
more than a leather-bound tome with golden pages.

I lift it carefully and look at
every corner of it.
It smells primordial,

like it has lived through centuries.
I place it before me and
open it carefully.

The letters on the pages glow,
dance, change, transform
before my very eyes.

And finally,
I begin to read
what I know is the ninth story.

The Ninth Story

Many years ago, there was a queen called Prasuti. She and her husband deeply desired a daughter. The Lord Brahma, aware of their plight, asked them to give up their royalty for a while and pray like saints to the Mahadevi, mother to us all.

The Mahadevi, upon being called with such fervour, awakened them from their prayers. She agreed to give them a daughter as they desired, but Prasuti, the queen, asked the Goddess to reincarnate herself as the child they desired. The Mahadevi warned them that should she ever be insulted, she would return to her home among the stars.

The couple agreed, and the Goddess was born again as Sati, a princess in the palace of Daksha and Prasuti. Brahma, who had done this by design as he wished Sati to marry Shiva, regaled the young princess with stories and legends of Shiva. They would reach her from the lips of courtiers and maids and sometimes even the Gods themselves.

So Sati fell in love with Shiva long before he even knew who she was. To win his heart, she gave up her luxuries and committed herself to a thousand rigorous penances. Her prayers were so intense that even the great Shiva could not resist her, and he fell in love with her as easily as he fell into meditation. Her father, King Daksha, a petty man, was completely against this union as Shiva, with his simple clothes and snakes and renunciation of luxuries, made him uncomfortable.

Still, Shiva and Sati were married, and she went to live with her husband in Kailash, his home.

King Daksha's ego was bruised, and in revenge, he planned a yagna ritual, and asked all the Gods, Goddesses and royalty to attend, other than his own daughter and her husband.

Sati, upon hearing of the yagna, decided to go. Shiva, however, refused to accompany her.

Instead of welcoming his daughter, King Daksha was furious. He told her coldly, 'You were not invited to the palace.'

Sati tried to comfort her father, told him she loved him. Nothing worked. Daksha grew angrier and angrier until he raised his voice. 'Get OUT! You are no daughter of mine.'

With those words, Sati's face darkened with fury. Her voice shook the palace walls. 'Do you not remember, oh King, who you speak to? I am no daughter of yours, I am the Goddess herself!'

She turned into her celestial form and began to wreak havoc across Daksha's palace, destroying everything in his kingdom and much, much beyond.

Daksha fell to his knees, begging forgiveness; even Prasuti prayed to the Goddess to stop. All the Gods tried to intervene. But it was too late. Sati denounced all her relationships, including the one with her husband, so nothing could bind her.

'Perhaps in my next birth I will be born to a father who I can respect and who respects me in return.' And she immolated her mortal body through ancient yogic power.

A grief-stricken Shiva, upon learning of Sati's death, rendered a dance of destruction that unleashed terror across the universe. He created a thousand malevolent deities to aid him with his destruction. The Earth burned. Planets exploded, stars died long before they were meant to. Many Gods, mortals and monsters perished.

After an age of destruction, Shiva, who was also all-forgiving, undid all his destruction and returned everything to its state before the Tandava. He then carried the body of his wife, in grief and sorrow, and roamed the universe. Lost without her.

Vishnu, who could not bear to see Shiva in such pain, as they were brothers after all, promised him peace and asked him to part with Sati's body. Her body was cut into fifty-one pieces, and the pieces fell upon the Earth, each one a new holy place to worship the Goddess.

After a long period, the Goddess was reborn as Parvati, a daughter of the Himalayan Mountains and devotee of Shiva. This time, she was born to a father who respected her husband. And when she was old enough, she married the Lord Shiva and ascended to being Parvati, the Goddess of Love, Devotion and Fertility.

This tale should end here.

But the tales of the Gods and Goddesses never do. You see, immortality is complicated. Reincarnation exists for this reason. The divine must walk with us through the ages. Every ninth century, the Gods and Goddesses reincarnate. For what good is a deity if they lose their ability to feel as deeply as humans do? What good is limitlessness if there is no reason to evolve or humble oneself anew?

When a Goddess reincarnates she doesn't remember who she was. Which is why it is the duty of the divine to tell her the stories. To give her guidance. To wake up the Goddess in her so she knows what she has to do. So she can wake the other reincarnated Gods too, as destiny and dharma calls them all. That is *you*.

This is your book.

The rest of these pages are yours to fill.

I Inhale Deeply

As so much falls into place …

Why the Goddesses have been visiting.
Shikhandi's lessons.
Ganesh seeming so familiar.
My love for the Tarot.
The poetry and the art.
Indra being named after the God of the Winds.
The wisdom and magic of Nani.
The kindness and wisdom of Mama.
Why I met Joy and Alexia.
Devon's tattoo.
Why he felt familiar, too.
The lessons I had to learn
from the pain.

This was why.
This was *why.*

Everyone calls me Paro,
but my name has always been Parvati.

The story is now
mine to tell.

Upasanhaar

Epilogue

Mama and I Go to Vaishno Devi

They do not visit me any more.
I know the journey is mine now.

But sometimes
I think I still see them.

In the corner of my eye,
I watch a flash of crimson and gold disappear.

I find a Ganesh murti at my window,
stone carved with glittering onyx eyes.

Ancient tales always find their way to me
when I need them the most.

I do not know what lies ahead.
But I do know I am not afraid.

I will meet it with courage in my heart
and a smile on my face,

You see, the first time I truly practise my magic,
it is under the mountain Goddess's care.

With my mother standing with me there,
I think of the day I may have a daughter,

and wonder if I would want her to be like me.
Part girl, part Goddess, full of stories.

So I pray to the divine mother in the sky,
the same one who held me close for so long.

I say, 'If I ever have a daughter,
please teach her the way you taught me.

Make her stronger than I ever was.
more clever and wise than I will ever be,

teach her how to be brave and truthful
about who you are, and how to live with grace.'

I say, 'If you do this for her,
she will become your daughter too.

Bless her the way you blessed me,
with divinity anew.'

Acknowledgements

With thanks to:

My parents, for always teaching me to stand up for myself and what I believe in.

My grandparents, for being an enduring testament to courage and survival.

My brother, for standing by me always.

Steve, for his heart.

Leopoldo, for his wild, creative spirit and generosity.

Nikesh, for being a force for good, and a champion of young authors and artists everywhere.

Niki, for being an absolute gem of a human being, a star of an agent, I could not have written this without you.

Trista, for being the friend and the editor this book and I needed, I cannot begin to express my gratitude to the hours and hours you have given this book child of mine.

Yena, for taking the time out to read and give me such excellent feedback.

Tristan and Joanna and Oscar, for always being kind and wonderful friends.

Emma, for her constant support, for being my editor, my friend and for helping me bring this special book to life.

Clare and Layla, you are both forever in my heart.

Dean Atta, Yrsa Daley Ward, Max Porter and all the brilliant writers who have written the beautiful verse novels and memoirs I have ever read.

Salena, Joelle, Brigitta, Nadine, Safiya, Salma, Carlos, Roger, Nerm, Sanah, Sophia, Anoushka, Shruti, Uzma, Susannah, Kate, Sim, Gaby – you constantly inspire me.

Alison, Shaun, Rebekah, Dave, Clara, Annie, Lauz, Emma, Heather, Matt, Faye – for your love and support.

And finally, to you dear reader. For joining me on this journey through story as style ... telling and family and growing up and perseverance and friendship and love and myth and finding who you are. The divine is within you too. I hope you find what you are looking for.

With verse, warmth and love,

Nikita